18.1.︎

To Stanley with [...]
wishes for [...]
returns

[illegible] N + M

Authority in a Changing Society

Authority in a Changing Society

edited by Clifford Rhodes

Constable London

First published in 1969
by Constable & Co Ltd
10 Orange Street, London WC2
Copyright © 1969 by Clifford Rhodes
All rights reserved
Printed in Great Britain
by The Anchor Press Ltd, Tiptree, Essex
SBN 09 455910 4

Contents

Introduction

It is not only from the young and rebellious in spirit that authority is under challenge. To interpret the contemporary mood of protest merely as an episode in the perennial war of the generations would be a blunder. The vitality of the young may urge them to greater vociferousness but it is highly questionable whether their discontent is any deeper than that of their elders.

Perhaps older people have better reason for dissatisfaction. They have had more experience. Each has his own list of particular grievances. Most of the causes of bitterness have been well aired by now in public discussion. But, apart from the personal scars we of the older generations have accumulated during the years, probably most of us feel a certain sadness and disillusion because the Wellsian visions of our youth have faded so badly. We may have been nurtured on the dreams of J. Addington Symonds:

> '*These things shall be! A loftier race*
> *Than e'er the world hath known shall rise*
> *With flame of freedom in their souls*
> *And light of science in their eyes.*
>
> *Nation with nation, land with land,*
> *Inarmed shall live as comrades free;*
> *In every heart and brain shall throb*
> *The pulse of one fraternity . . .*'

and so on.

Loftier, certainly, the race has become, with an inch or two added to average physical stature. It may even be regarded as a moral advance that the individual has a wider range of choices than ever before. More than that, increased knowledge has broadened the kindliness and sympathy of ordinary men

7

and women, particularly towards children and the unfortunates and misfits of society. The attitudes of the makers and administrators of the law have changed fundamentally towards criminals, particularly those of tender age, towards the conduct of personal relations and towards questions of personal morality. What Lord Stow Hill has written on the subject in this symposium could hardly have come from the pens of his predecessors of a century ago in the offices he has held. These gains are invaluable although they are often overlooked. But, in the minds of many people, the debit side of the balance sheet swamps them. The personal frustration, the impoverishment of human relationships, the economic insecurity, the plight of the aged, the lack of purpose, the superficiality and the feverishness of life, the perpetual threat of destruction, the meaninglessness of affluence: all this does not indicate that our own nation has lost an empire without gaining a role but that technological society has gained a world and lost its soul.

Because this discontent is vague and ill-defined nobody knows where to strike or what to reform. Discontent therefore looks for an easy target and finds it in 'faceless bureaucracy' or the alleged hypocrisy of politicians. In the pubs and clubs men call for the reconstruction of the Civil Service or for a system of referendums or for a government of businessmen or for an end to party politics and the appointment of a coalition: dreary nostrums that will not bear a moment's examination. Change and reform there must always be as a continuous process of adjustment to a perpetually changing situation. But salvation will not be found in this or that political reform or in this or that piece of legislation. The social evils of the last century could be adequately dealt with by such measures as the Reform Acts, the Factory Acts and trade union legislation. The problem now is much more subtle and complex. Political action is only one factor among many. The present discontents will find their solution, if at all, only over a long period by the theorising of philosophers and theologians, the planning of economists, the creativity of artists, the insights of poets, the policies of statesmen, the writing of literary men and, in fact, a general advance over the broadest possible front.

It is not surprising that the young and impatient should want

a more dramatic programme than this, without necessarily
knowing what it is to be. To the cynicism many of them have
inherited from their elders is added a sense of being a Tantalus
at the mercy of a society whose smooth promises recede as soon
as they reach out to take them at their word. During the past
quarter-century a serious mistake has been made in discounting
as the activities of a lunatic fringe the various asocial movements that have followed one after another: teddy boys, mods
and rockers, beats, hippies, flower children, C.N.D. and the
like. These movements have for many been the only available
means of protest against the suffocation and frustration they
have experienced. They have been symptomatic of a desire to
find a new identity and a new way of life that is very widespread
among an age-group that, as the cohesive force of the family
has been whittled away, has more than ever experienced a
sense of its common interests and solidarity. There have been
attempts to devise a new and relevant morality to replace the
traditional morality that has seemed to them hypocritical and
out of touch with reality.

As would be expected, when the mood of protest seized the
universities it became more articulate and more activist. Precise
demands were formulated. In different countries similar conditions produced a similar mood but the manifestations of discontent and the actual demands differed from one university
to another. It was clear enough that the students were no more
sure of what would really solve their problems than anybody
else. In general their demands boiled down to a claim for
participation in university government which, whatever the
position may have been in France and elsewhere, in this
country could make little difference of any consequence to anything. Student leaders came out with statements that their
education should be regarded as a right and not a privilege;
that they were protesting against 'society in general' – which is
rather like declining to accept the universe – and that they
were against '*the* system', without specifying to what elements
in which system they objected.

Naturally, my mind returns nostalgically to my own under-
graduate experience in the thirties and to what my contemporaries were saying and thinking. I remember it as a period

of my life when, more than ever before or since, I could – and did – do as I pleased. Discipline was too light to be irksome and liberty was maximal. I do not recollect anybody regarding his presence at Oxford either as a privilege or a right. We thought of it more as an opportunity, carrying with it a duty, to obtain the training that would make the most of such abilities as we possessed and to prepare ourselves for the future. There was much discussion as to whether Oxford was an 'end in itself'. We were on excellent terms of equality and friendship with our tutors who were always willing to guide us along such of the leafy lanes of academic enquiry as interested us. In discussion with them we had considerable influence in arranging our own programmes of studies and the curriculum offered enough options to satisfy the widest ranging of minds. The idea that any of us could have gained anything by protests, sit-ins or demonstrations never occurred to us. If crowds gathered in the streets it was usually to watch some bold athlete climbing to the top pinnacle of the Martyr's Memorial or to celebrate the foiling of Guy Fawkes. We would have laughed at the notion that we should waste our very precious time electing student representatives to sit uselessly on the Hebdomadal Council, if we even knew what that austere assembly was. And utterly useless that kind of representation must surely be. The Vice-Chancellor of York University deals with the point in this volume.

This did not mean that we were oblivious of the wickedness of the world or that we lived in ivory towers. Indeed, the ills of humanity pressed upon us more unavoidably than they do upon students now. The queues of unemployed and destitute, the desperation of Jarrow and the dereliction of the coalfields were ever present with us. The rickety legs and pinched faces of undernourished children, comparatively rare nowadays, were a constant reminder of meaningless suffering. Some men went off to fight against Franco. Abyssinia was as much a horror to us as Vietnam. We cared passionately about these evils. But we would never for a moment have imagined that we could disperse them by marching and demonstrating. We hoped to do better by turning our training to good account as an instrument for dealing with them when our time came. This was the heyday of student political clubs. We were forming our minds and forging our weapons. I find that most of the young people in my own circle of acquaintances today still take a similar attitude and surely it is not an unintelligent one.

Perhaps that was a golden age of universities. It may be that a university such as I knew is inconceivable under present-day conditions, although by all accounts the new universities founded since the war are highly enlightened. But it has to be recognised that modern, computerised civilisation, with its vast populations crammed into small areas, has raised entirely new problems of administration in all fields. The base of the social pyramid has been greatly enlarged but the apex is still, by geometrical necessity, a single point. If communications break down and if healthy dialogue between governors and governed is stultified, that is understandable. Marches and demonstrations can then be seen as a crude and terribly imprecise attempt to improve the situation. The protest is not so much against authority as against the failure of communication on both sides. This is the province of the press and of the media of mass communication, to say nothing of the specialists in public relations. Indeed those in control of these agencies strive manfully to establish a two-way traffic in ideas: but in the end it is impossible to develop genuine conversation. Always in the last resort the few are addressing the many – and 'telling' them. Even when they try to enter into the public mind by the pitiably inadequate method of the opinion polls it is still 'they' who ask the questions. The relation of the administrator to the administered is that of subject and object. The ordinary citizen never feels himself to be in a relation of personal confrontation.

Since, then, the protest movement both among young and old is so ill-formulated and its objectives so ill-defined, a useful approach to the problems it raises would be to take a good look at the authorities against which it is directed. Behind every 'impersonal system' and every 'faceless bureaucracy' there are, in fact, persons with faces. What do they consider to be their true functions? How do they think? How do their minds work? What inner struggles and conflicts disturb them? How do they themselves see their responsibilities? When they have dealt with the questions of journalists and interviewers what kind of questions do they ask of themselves in moments of crisis or emergency? In the nature of things, few of those who are casting upon them the blame for our present discontents can have any deep insight into all of this. There is only one way to find out: ask the people in authority themselves.

It is in that spirit that this volume has been compiled. We are not here interested so much in the forms and structures of authority as in what happens within them and how they are used. The forms and structures can be studied in the academic textbooks of comparative politics and administration. This is not said in the exasperated spirit of Pope:

> '*For forms of government let fools contest,*
> *What e'er is best administered is best.*'

Forms are not by any means without importance. Yet we may have the finest machinery of democracy imaginable but unless the people operating it are actuated by the right motives and principles it will avail us nothing. To that extent Pope was right. During the twelve or eighteen months since the plan of this volume was first conceived the issues have become steadily more insistent.

I invited leaders in various fields of national activity to tell us about their experience of the exercise of high authority and what they had learned from it that was relevant to the present situation. All the contributors have more than fulfilled this commission. Through all that they have written there is revealed something of their self-questioning; their feeling of respect for personality; their conviction that authority, rightly understood, does not mean power but service; that dialogue with their constituents must be continuous; that they should not impose their authority but carry people with them.

But the person holding authority should always be leader as well as servant, if only because he is better informed and more experienced than those he serves. By what standards and to what destination does he lead? This question is crucial because it may well be the rejection of traditional attitudes to standards and values that is at the root of our troubles. Roger Holmes, writing on 'The Psychology of Authority', describes the transition that is taking place in this respect and suggests that it is to be welcomed. All transitions are difficult.

The Archbishop of York is able to claim that his own title to exercise authority resides in the fact that he himself is under an authority higher than human. This makes an absolute demand upon him and prescribes the standards he must observe. In this case the mode of his appointment, whether by election or nomination, is a secondary consideration. In the name of the higher authority he is justified in making a stand if he believes it to be necessary even against those who have put him where he is. In this conviction, churchmen under totalitarian régimes have dared openly to defy the whole power of the State itself with all its apparatus of terrorism. It is a conviction that rests upon belief in the divine transcendence. Theologians who rest their case on the divine immanence, to the neglect or denial of transcendence, and who look for the God within, are in a much less strong position. If they are right every individual can say with justification, 'I am God'. Follow the logical development of this and every man's judgment becomes as valid as anybody else's, which is democracy run mad and the apotheosis of mediocrity. In any case, nobody really believes it.

Nowadays it is the minority, only, who are able to accept the position taken by the Archbishop in its fulness. The late C. G. Jung dug deeply into the fundamental reasons for the incapacity of the majority to enter into the religious universe of discourse. Because of it, many people look to science rather than to religion as the source of truth. They accept its authority the more gladly because it passes the most convincing of tests: 'it works'. Also, the knowledge it has gained assists in the solution of a number of troublesome ethical problems even if, in the process of doing so, it raises a host of new ones. People are impressed because scientists acknowledge a value beyond the immediate and the material, that of truth, which they serve with dedication. Sir Bernard Lovell, however, tells us that the issue is not as simple as that. Scientific method can never answer the ultimate questions and works more in terms of fact than of value. Nor can scientists any longer follow the direction indicated by their own researches. They, too, are under authority, but not now the authority of reason and truth only, but of the lay controllers of finance who ordain from the stand-point of military, industrial or social need what enquiries they shall undertake. Truth for its own sake is giving place to technology for the sake of utility. To the question, 'useful for what?', the answer only too often has to be, 'for the service of public caprice'.

Since authority cannot any longer justify its actions by reference to absolute standards, it has to become more than ever the servant of the public. In doing so, paradoxically perhaps, it participates in the most obviously free and spontaneous of public activities and is welcomed there. However unpopular particular decisions may be, nobody resents the principle of leadership in sport, for example, and all sportsmen recognise that the rules, the law, are in fact the game. Without them there would be no game. Both Sir Stanley Rous, dealing with sport, and Lady Reading, on the subject of voluntary organisations, show how authority functions as support, protection and safe-guard. It does not infringe the liberty of the participants but guarantees it. Carry the same thought through its logical development and we arrive at the function of government itself. When government ceases to fulfil that function, then is the time to rush to the barricades. Lady Sharp describes how urgently our own civil administration strives to ensure that it shall be fulfilled. How far interference is justified, she writes, is an ever-present question. Much of the continual carping at the alleged sins of Whitehall is ill-informed and prejudiced. There are occasions when Whitehall does, in undeniable fact, 'know best'. If it did not there would indeed be ground for complaint. In spite of that, the visage of the typical civil servant is not furrowed with the pangs of power hunger.

At the opposite end of the scale to voluntary associations stands the military institution, surely the most autocratically governed of all. Obedience is a *sine qua non* of military efficiency. Yet the main difference is in the tightness of the discipline and the strength of the sanctions behind it. Even in voluntary associations there has to be discipline and always there are sanctions. This apart, it is astonishing to note how the statements of General Sir John Hackett and Lady Reading gear in with each other. The military life is necessarily a well ordered life: yet when this orderliness is properly understood and accepted, and when the autocratic authority of the military commander is properly exercised, the serving soldier does not find them oppressive or restrictive but liberating. This emphasises the truth that freedom is grounded in law and authority.

That is why the case for anarchism breaks down at every point. The question is not whether we ought to submit to law and authority but to what kind of law and authority we ought to submit. Anarchism means the free licensing of the bully and the spiv.

I hope and believe that this collection of writings will assist in clarifying some of the issues that are disturbing all thoughtful people at the present time. Certainly they have helped me, personally, and I have learned much in the process of collecting them together. Perhaps if I had known at the beginning what a volume of work I should be involved in my courage would have been daunted by the task. If any readers should feel that more fields of activity should have been included I shall not quarrel with the criticism but shall plead in extenuation that to have included all that ought to have been included would have made the book unwieldy and the problem of assembling and editing it quite unmanageable.

My compensation – and more than compensation – has been the pleasure I have had in the friendliness and co-operativeness of the team of contributors. They have spared neither time nor trouble. I should like to express publicly the gratitude I have offered them privately and to thank them most warmly. There are many others who have assisted and advised me to whom I owe thanks, but to mention them all by name would require too long a list. Mr. Benjamin Glazebrook, of Constable, cannot be omitted. Not only did he see the possibilities of this book at my first approach but subsequently allowed me to carry on with it without the least interference. In this instance, at least, as my own 'authority', he has fulfilled the ideal. Any experienced editor will know what I mean.

Clifford Rhodes

May 1968

Roger Holmes

Lecturer in Social Psychology,
London School of Economics

Any full discussion of the nature of authority must bring up issues which are part personal, part social, and part transcendental. The third of these aspects, that of the final value of any accepted external guidance in matters of faith and conduct, cannot be within my purview. This is an issue that I would not, as a psychologist, presume to judge. All I can do in that capacity (and it is as a psychologist that I speak in this paper) is to outline what I believe to be some of the individual and social concomitants of such beliefs.

These two aspects – the personal and the social – are very closely interlinked. In any discussion of the individual we must consider the society into which he is embedded and in any discussion of society we must consider the nature of the individuals that compose it. Since not everything can be said at once and as I must start somewhere I shall begin with the individual. Later, I shall relate what I have said to the wider social scene. For reasons that should become apparent, I shall take the development in two stages.

The basis of our relations with authority are laid down in the very earliest years of our life and it is there that we must begin our account. For, to a very large extent, our individual characters are formed by the resolution of that most crucial and earliest of personal affronts – our confrontation with that germ of authority – that which is bigger than the self. This confrontation, which must happen in the first months of life, destroys forever our primary illusion of solitude and omnipotence. Although the term 'omnipotence' may sound bizarre when applied to the small infant, we must remember that a sense of
16

The Psychology of Authority

power can be derived not only from a conquest of that which is seen to be outside the self, but also quite as much by the lack of anything that could refute such an assumption. It is omnipotence in this second, negative, sense that is our psychological ground.

The only first reality is the self; being unaware of what we cannot do, we feel we can do all. What destroys this illusion is the dawning awareness of powers external to the self, most strikingly, but not necessarily solely, exemplified by the existence of our parents. Our parents not only constrict us in that they order our existence and so conflict with our desires: they reinforce our sense of smallness and dependence. We feel ourselves dependent – what could possibly be a greater affront to our primitive narcissism? – upon that which appears arbitrary and, above all, mysterious. This sense of 'mystery' is crucial. Forced to accommodate to that which the child has no means of rationally 'understanding', the child absorbs the parents into his magical world: the parent is 'idealised', and seen as larger than life, the father (or perhaps, more importantly, the mother) part of a framework in which the only determinant is the will. The parent is now seen as omnipotent, beyond good and evil, arbitrary and incomprehensible. How the child copes with this eruption of the uncontrolled in very large measure determines his emotional outlook for life.

The child accommodates to the incomprehensible by 'identifying' with the parent. The demands of the parents are 'introjected' by the child; he makes them his own. The parent, rather than remaining outside, is 'internalised' as conscience and the first phase of adaptation to the world of others has occurred.

Two points are relevant here. In the first place, the process is by no means without conflict. A residual resentment of that which disturbs our peace remains. We remain 'ambivalent' to that which we cannot control. This remaining resentment is of the utmost importance and I shall return to it in a moment. In the second place, the child renders the accommodation to some extent acceptable to himself by squaring the circle and gaining a sense of vicarious control. The child can do this by identifying, not with the parent herself, but with the values which are implicit in the parent's prescription. When the parent insists that the child washes his hands before meals, for instance, she may well do so in shocked tones – 'Wash your hands before meals, what will people think?' The child can see that the parent too is in awe, for the parent too has been a child and is beset by a yet higher authority. And so the opportunity arises of the child taking unto himself not just the dictates of the parents but of the standards which these prescriptions exemplify. Immediately a form of equality is struck, for were the parents now to come to meals with dirty hands, the child could in all justice say, 'But Mummy, you told us only to eat with clean hands.' The force of this (usually unsaid) riposte is, 'What will "people" think of *you?*' The parent, too, is subordinate: the higher authority, 'people', has been brought in to make the parent and child equal before the bar of a still higher tribunal, which is in this case public opinion, but could be 'the authorities' or 'the powers that be'.

The child will identify, then, more readily with those who are themselves identified. The child's ambivalence remains. The child is in effect saying, 'I will only identify with your demands provided you too pay the price, provided you too are not omnipotent and subscribe to a yet higher code.' The price of our submission, then, is the submission of others.

In itself this first development can account for vast areas of adult morality and, indeed, wider social living, for the attitude towards the parent generalises in later life to all forms of inevitable, arbitrary dictates. The parent is replaced by the king, the law courts and the priest – anyone that forces him into a dependent, subordinate position – but the similarity will remain. The adult too will identify with the *status quo* and take its dictates as sacrosanct provided those above him do so as well.

Whole areas of social living can thus become 'moralised', legitimated in and of themselves, held to be of value and so beyond question and use.

It is at this point, indeed, that we can relate the psychology of the individual to that of the society at large. By the workings of its earliest psychological mechanism, whole societies may become overgrown by a ritual morality that allows each a narcissistic victory and the sense of mystery and of solitary power fulfilled.

Such a society I shall call a 'society of value', for acts will now be valued, not for their consequences – this is crucial – but for their conformity to pre-established principle. All forms of assertive, idiosyncratic individualism in such a society will be decried: the craftsman, the king and the priest will not pursue their vocations for private gain but because they believe they do what they do for the public's sake. The craftsman's 'pride' will be involved in doing good work, the king, and most particularly the priest, will serve 'the community' and the authorities reflected therein. Each will value the other for each will be playing a part in the other's private world of power.

Such a society will have dignity and a sense of organic continuity. This is attractive: but before advocating a return to the days when such societies did in fact exist – when the craftsman at Chartres was content to dedicate his work to God and was prepared to leave it out of sight to other's eyes – we should bear in mind that it has certain serious drawbacks. Such a society will of its very nature be static and conservative. Change will be greeted as impiety, for to do something new is to violate the self-denying compact we have made with our fellows. It will almost certainly be hierarchical, for it will of its inner nature be a reflection of that first inequality of the parent and child. Not just the 'what', the 'who' may be legitimated; that is, denied the possibility of choice. Laws of succession, just as much as any other laws, may become moralised, and where succession has become sacred it is sacrilege to usurp.

Such a society may well give us good government – at least, by the unexacting standards of the permitted; for the leader's task will be simple and he will not be threatened. His task will be simple for, in essence, it will be the maintenance of the *status quo*. 'What' should be done is not in doubt: the only possible doubt lies in the 'how', and that too will come to be prescribed. He will not be threatened for others may have no hope of legitimately supplanting him. He may thus treat his subordinates, divided by class and caste as they may be, in an odd sense as equals: equals before the bar of higher duty. It is just this quality of profound equality that so recommends it to the subordinate.

But such a society has never existed. 'Legitimacy' is probably never wholly absent from any society – not for long anyway, since sheer continuity permits the ever-continued moral growth of precedence – but it is never present in such a concentrated form as here described. For one thing the rulers may not behave themselves. Finding themselves in positions of power they may well use their positions for personal gain, reserving their moral stances (like some managers in industry with their appeal to the 'loyalty' of their staff) for conditions when the subordinates need to be kept under control. For another thing, such a society of value may well fail when pitted against a more pragmatic rival. Finally, important as the first five years of life may be, they are not the whole story.

A crucial development occurs at about the age of four or five. The child begins to play in a co-operative way with what the psychologists call his 'peers', those of the same age as himself. Before this, the child's meaningful relations were mainly with his parents; a child of three may show a passionate interest in his younger brother, but only because the younger brother has usurped his position as youngest child. At about four or five he will come to play with his fellows for its own sake. A new form of relationship is born – that of dealing with our equals.

This relationship is different from the relationship he has with his parents in one crucial respect, namely that he shares the same world. Two five-year-olds have more in common in their interests and their problems than they could ever have with their parents, however loving these parents may be. To the child, much of the parents' behaviour must appear (as already noted) a 'mystery'. Indeed, the form of morality that is a legacy of the earlier period reflects that which must always appear to be arbitrary to those who are weak and cannot understand.

This is by no means the case with his friends. Here he shares the same framework and as a result can 'empathise' – share the feelings of those that have shared his dilemmas. But he can do more than share the feelings of others; he can come to 'understand' and to see the other as acted *upon*. What do we mean when we say, 'I can see your point of view', but that 'I am aware of the pressures you have to contend with'? Indeed any true knowledge of the other must be of this form, an acknowledgement of common lot.

Gone now are the mysterious fiats we avow but can never understand, fiats that we accept with resentment and seek to impose upon superior and inferior alike. In its stead we find a different form of morality. The 'morality of principle', as we might call it, is replaced by the 'morality of concern'. For where we can understand, where we can see that the other too is driven by circumstance and not by some feared inner anarchic impulse, there can we abandon our rival desire for mastery and become more tolerant. Furthermore, moral observations will no more be in the form of an *a priori*, 'thou shalt not kill', for instance, which is immune to circumstance, but will depend more upon the very circumstance that illuminates them. Viewed from this second point of view, the desirability of killing the other will depend upon context and consequence: given the chance, someone should have killed Hitler in 1933.

This later development can also provide the basis for the wider social living of later years. For the later, adult society may not just be founded on value, it may also be founded on relativity. Relativity can have its disadvantages as well as advantages and, perhaps somewhat unfairly, I shall call the 'pure case' of such a later derivation the 'society of use'.

For such a society can become almost too flexible. Rational thought can never tell us what to do, it can only tell us how. In the placing of events in their context, as the child at this age learns to do, he learns the language of relativity and science – but he also by the same token learns to dilute the notion of an inherent property. Events, people and objects will come to be valued not for what they 'are' but what they 'do'. Whole areas of our social living may become infected by a corroding pragmatism that allows none of the consolation of the unquestioned:

goods may be made for use and be no better than they have to be; friends will be made in order to be influenced, and morality will become a matter of calculation and degree.

The shortcomings of such a 'society of use' do not end there. The greatest casualty of all, there can be no doubt, will be authority itself. The notion of authority, in any meaningful permanent sense, will find itself under attack. The leader will be less accepted (since he could in principle be supplanted) at the very moment when his task, that of making creative decisions in an evolving situation, becomes one of infinitely greater difficulty. The guardians of continuity will themselves be called into question.

But such a 'society of use' has never existed either, not at least in the extreme form as described here. Pragmatism, like committal, is nearly always a matter of degree. The static yard-stick of value has been overthrown again and again by the manifest advantages of an alternative course of action, but such innovations have in turn been absorbed by the legitimacy that is granted to that which has latterly come to be accepted. The war chariot proved superior to the foot soldier: mounted cavalry proved superior to the chariot: each in turn was revered and each in turn was finally superseded.

In our personal relations we manifest an equally complex ambivalence of orientation. Most individuals are men both of principle and concern. Of concern to those they can understand, their immediate circle of friends, and of principle thereafter – in their attitudes to the alien they do not know and to the criminal whose sole motivation must appear as wilful revolt. The wider society in particular has probably always been articulated by the inflexible demands of principle, particularly as exemplified in the notion of 'legitimacy' in the assertion of rights and duties.

Is there, then, nothing more to be said? Are the problems that confront us today but age-old problems in a more acute form? In a sense this is of course true, and yet in another sense it is not. And to do justice to the contemporary scene and the status of authority within it I shall have to take a closer look at what is happening today.

In part, our current society looks like an extreme caricature of the 'society of use'. With innovations confronting us on every side, nothing would appear to be free from the sanction of failure. Leadership positions have largely been thrown open to all: anyone, whatever his birth, can achieve eminence, and so can, in turn, be superseded or shown to be out of date. What should be done, and how, are both doubted. Leaders like the rest find no guidance in continuity.

All is called into question and this approach has gone further than before in one area of peculiar importance. With advances in medical science, dogmas which have been totally un-questioned for centuries, at least in principle if not in practice, have been thrown into doubt. Is human life always sacred? Are we always right to preserve a form of life in the old, as we can so often do these days, rather than allow them the surcease that would come from painless death? What of the thalidomide baby? What of the unconceived child and the problem of birth control?

These problems are not only important in their direct im-plications; what, for example, would be the consequences of being able to specify the type of child one wished, for instance. They are also important for what might be termed their 'side-effects' on the position of the current authorities, such as they remain. Possibly nothing is doing the Roman Catholic Church more harm at the moment, for instance, or causing more avoid-able human misery, than its indecision on the matter of birth control. With the coming of ethical choice where none before existed, the very guardians of our morality, of their essence stable and committed to 'eternal' truths, are themselves being 'shown up' *for this very reason*. Those who claim they are always right can never admit to being wrong.

Lest this account seem too gloomy, it must also be stressed that the very knowledge that has given the choice and doubt has also in many ways given us tolerance and compassion. The old morality of principle was all too often heartless in the purity of its concern. The criminal, the homosexual, and the insane are far less cruelly treated than they were.

Yet none of these considerations, whether good or bad – the exploitation of 'use', the dilution of religious authority and the growth of compassion – really express what is qualitatively new in our scene. The hallmark of our age is not revolt, which has happened often enough in the past, but sheer indifference. In this sense, the society of use really has gone further than ever before. *Authority is no longer even attacked*; this is the crucial development, this is the qualitative jump of recent times. In the past there were rebels but they were rebels of principle. Like Luther, they castigated the Pope, not for being Christian, but for not being Christian enough. The rebel was intensely conservative, the most intolerant man of all. There was nothing else he could be. But now a new turn of events has occurred, a development that largely accounts for our concern for the young. This is not that of the revolt against the Establishment: it is the disappearance of the Establishment into irrelevance and absurdity. The sheep do not look up for they are not interested in being fed. Even the Queen, the quintessential symbol of the Establishment, is no longer attacked: she is just ignored.

How has this come about? It has come about because it is now possible, as it never was before, to escape. The young, and indeed all of us, can escape because we can move from the environment of our youth and the restraints upon us that still re-echo therein. But we can even, if we would, escape at home. Society, as a result of technical advance, is now so fragmented that each may well be ignorant of his neighbour's role. We can no longer observe, let alone decry.

But the young cannot only escape supervision and hence free themselves from the enforcement of that principle to which they were in earlier times so readily subject, they can also escape dependence. As never before, they have attained financial autonomy and have become a consumer group in their own right. As a result they have gained the identity of an economic unit, with their own patterns of consumption and choice. This is what is so new. The young have formed their own society, a society not modelled on their elders'. It is a society without the superstructure of enforceable law; it is an informal, personal society, a society that rejects the continuity of the past and is more than usually a prey to the dictates of craze and fashion – but is nonetheless a potent social force for all that.

Short of unforeseen cataclysm, such as mass starvation, with a resulting concentration of political power amongst men of principle who enforce their beliefs by scientific means they secretly despise, these developments seem likely to stay. The opportunism of commerce and the accommodation to the deviant are both likely to remain – and so will the indifference of youth. It may be that a reverence for life itself will go, but, if it does, it seems far more likely to result from overpopulation than from excessive pragmatism – an overpopulation that is being at the moment actively encouraged by the absolutes of nationalism and religion. What seems a more likely casualty of the present development is any sense of corporate, organic social unity, whether nationalistic, professional or religious, with its glorious, self-sufficient implications of a return to a primitive narcissism. But even if this is so it is by no means necessarily to be bemoaned. The old organic sense of unity was ultimately, when all is said and done, based on power and the resentful acceptance of that which was then demanded of others. Respect for authority as such, the ideological buttress of power, will go too. We may come to live in a cynical and an irreverent age but it need not be a vindictive one. Sexual freedom is surely far less noxious than cruelty in the name of an ideal.

These developments have of course affected the whole of society, not just the young. The older may fret and feel that loss of power that inevitably follows when their values are decried, but they too have been affected nonetheless. We are all of us more permissive, less doctrinaire and decided than we were – but we evince as well that greater tolerance and genuine concern for the other that comes with deeper understanding. We are all of us 'used' and commercially exploited: but we all enjoy the personal freedom and choice that such an exploitation can imply.

Society, too, despite these advances, remains well ordered, with arguably sufficient structure for its maintenance and growth. In an odd sort of way, we have struck a balance between pragmatism and principle that should not wholly be deplored. At least, and indeed it may be thought excessively so, we are a society that permits within itself the possibility of change. All change is painful, for it affronts the continuity we have made our own, but none of us should be so complacent of the old rigidities that we should willingly advocate their wholesale return.

Is all then to the good? Oddly enough the most serious casualties of the present developments can be seen as the young themselves; the very section of the population that has been most emancipated. For their position is still ambiguous. They can order their lives as never before, but they still have to come to terms with a situation where the vast preponderance of positions of power and influence are held by those older then themselves. They still have to accommodate and take jobs, to obey those they may very well not respect. Perhaps this is inevitable, given the age-structure of society and the necessary allocation of responsibilities to those with greater experience, but for all that the sense of constriction and helplessness remains. This may account in part for the use to which they put their new-found freedom, for their withdrawal into phantasy and solitude, and their stress on clothes and drugs, which are the fancy dress of the child at play and the solitary opiate of those who cut themselves off, or are cut off, from the public world of formal power.

So much for my thesis. I began by describing two 'pure cases' – that based on the acceptance of principle where there was no escape and that based on the relativity of choice. Both were 'pure cases' and neither has probably ever existed in its full form: 'principle' was confronted by failure, relativity gave us not just greater insight and tolerance (when presented to us as knowledge) but also, when commercially exploited, of economic choice. If the former can give us the 'glory' of national victory and the 'meaningfulness' of a corporately owned organic continuity, the latter can give us a more truly idiosyncratic individuality.

But what of the exercise of authority? That too may go – at least as we have known it so far. It may have lost forever its aura of inevitability. Allegiance may have to be won, not by the reiteration of timeless principle but by the manifest need for something to be done. It will probably be far easier to get young people to volunteer to help for Shelter or Oxfam than it will be to get them into the army or even into church. Whether this development is considered desirable or undesirable is for the reader to decide, but, in deciding, let him not be influenced by the envy he may feel for those who are younger than he is and have had a greater chance to escape.

The Most Rev. and Right Hon. F. D. Coggan, D.D.

Anyone who attempts even to begin a consideration of the subject of authority in religion and in the Church can hardly start elsewhere than with the Gospels. If he approaches the earliest of the four, the Gospel according to St. Mark, he meets the subject in the very first chapter. As Jesus taught in the synagogue on the Sabbath, the thing that astounded his hearers was that, 'unlike the doctors of the Law, He taught with a note of *authority*'.

This, combined with his healing of the man with convulsions, made the people exclaim: 'What is this? A new kind of teaching! He speaks with *authority* . . .' (St. Mark i, 21–8). They were accustomed to the teaching which derived its authority from the number or eminence of those who could be quoted in its favour – 'Rabbi A. in the name of Rabbi B. in the name of Rabbi C. says . . .; but Rabbi X. in the name of Rabbi Y. in the name of Rabbi Z. says . . .'. But here was one who quite clearly had an authority of His own. 'You have learned what our forefathers were told. . . . But what *I* tell you is this . . .' (St. Matthew v, 21 ff.). This was, indeed, something startlingly new, incisive in its demands on conscience, imperious in its call for obedience.

This question of the authority of Jesus was not something to be debated as a matter of mere curiosity – as it were at arm's length. When the chief priests, lawyers and elders, puzzled by the activities of Jesus, came to him and said, 'By what authority are you acting like this? Who gave you authority to act in this way?' (St. Mark xi, 27 ff.), He gave them no straight answer. He simply asked an embarrassing question of *them* – one they dared not answer – and sent them away with a blank refusal

28

to debate at no depth an issue which He could see (though they could not) impinged on heart and will, on conscience and action.

No; the question of authority was, for Jesus, not primarily a subject for intellectual debate. It was a matter which touched the very roots of His own religious conviction. When He taught men about the Kingdom of God – and this would seem clearly to have been the main theme of his teaching – He was not one lecturing with academic detachment *de Deo*. He was in a very real sense drawing aside the curtain of His own spiritual experience, sharing with His hearers the secret of what God's authority over Him meant. The Reign of God, the authority of God, this was a reality with which He had to come to terms every day of His life – at least from the adolescent realisation that He must be about His Father's business to the day when, having cried, 'Not My will but Thine be done', He could say, 'Father, into Thy hands I commend my spirit'.

The point I am trying to make is this: the unique authority of Jesus, seen alike in His teaching and His acts of power, seen, noted and marvelled at by His contemporaries, this authority was His precisely because He Himself was under authority. He knew, as no one else before or since has known, what it means to do always those things that pleased the Father. 'I do nothing on My own authority, but in all that I say, I have been taught by My Father' (St. John viii, 28). Whether these words be the *ipsissima verba* of Jesus or, to use William Temple's phrase, 'the interpretative recollection of a memory', they convey the truth of the point at issue.

It was from this basic position of personal religion that Jesus proceeded in His teaching work and especially in His training of the Twelve and other disciples. What He had learned of the authority of God, what He was continually learning in His daily religious experience, *that* He must seek to impart to them. It would not be easy. To communicate a system, to teach them a set of rules, to inculcate a series of directions, this would be a simple matter. But this would not do – not if He were going to produce men of authority who themselves were under divine authority. He must treat them as adults, not children. He must, as T. W. Manson used to say, give them direction rather than directions. This might often prove tantalising to them, even annoying. He would often have to refuse to give a straight answer to a straight question, and that is always annoying if you want to be saved the bother of thinking a thing out for yourself. 'What do you think'? He would say, and then counter their question with another, or answer their question with a story which made them think much more deeply than they had done when they posed the original question.

'The Spirit of the Lord is upon Me'; He had read the words from Isaiah 61 on that first Sabbath of His public ministry in the synagogue at Nazareth (St. Luke iv, 16 ff.). The Spirit – the wind; who was to say where it would blow? Who could measure its power or predict its direction? Try to contain it, and you may look very silly as you see your puny efforts in ruins at your feet. But put yourself in the way of it, set your sail to catch it, place yourself under its authority, and you may find yourself an instrument of power far greater than yourself. Jesus' ministry was to be a demonstration of precisely that. It was thus that He would be enabled to teach, to preach, to heal, to reach right judgments, to rise to increasing demands, to be stretched and not to break. He would try to train His men along similar lines. He would show them what divine authority really meant.

Such training would call for a radical recasting on their part of their value judgments. They had been brought up to think of authority in terms of power. 'In the world the recognised rulers lord it over their subjects, and their great men feel the weight of authority' (Mark x, 42). True enough! If they wanted evidence of that, they had only to look around them and see it working out in the domination of the whole Roman system. But – 'that is not the way with you; among you, whoever wants to be great must be your servant, and whoever wants to be first must be the willing slave of all'. This was a revolution in the concept of authority! And the revolution was so radical that it would seem it could not take effect in their thinking until, the passion of Jesus being past and the Holy Spirit having been given, they could work it out in the light of that event and in the power of the Paraclete.

This initial glance at the subject of authority as it presents itself to us in the Gospels – and space does not allow for more than this – suggests some valuable lines of guidance for those whose task it is to exercise authority in the Church of God. 'Take thou authority to exercise the office of a deacon in the Church of God . . .', says the bishop to the man kneeling before him. 'Take thou authority to preach the Word of God, and to minister the Holy Sacraments . . .', says the bishop to the man being ordained priest. And, though the language used in the consecration of a bishop is different, the idea of authority recurs both in the prayers and in the words used by the arch-bishop when he hands a Bible to the newly consecrated bishop.

The subject of the kind of authority exercised by the clergy is one of great concern to the most sensitive of their number, particularly in a day when there is a general dis-ease about any kind of authority and when in many circles the very idea of it is resented. 'What right have I,' the curate or vicar may ask, 'to preach to these people Sunday by Sunday? Many of them are better educated than I am; very many of them far more experienced in life and affairs. Who am I to harangue them?' He does well to ask such questions and to ask them sincerely. Who indeed is he? Who am I? But if he can find no answer to these questions it will go ill with him and with his ministry. Authority matters.

He must surely begin to find his answer along the lines suggested by our brief study of the Gospels. Our Lord's words and acts derived their authority from the fact that our Lord Himself was under authority. Here is our first and absolutely fundamental principle. He alone can preach who knows him-self, in the depths of his spiritual life, to be a man under domination, the reign of God Himself. There is a hand on his shoulder directing him and he is supremely contented to live his life, so far as he knows how, under that direction. In fact, his great ambition is to be able to approximate his Master in saying, 'I do always those things that please Him'. The Spirit of the Lord is upon him, and his aim is so to set his sail as to catch the Wind. Unless this is a reality – the great reality of his life – he may read his people an essay Sunday by Sunday, he may give them a few good thoughts drawn from the papers with a dash of scripture added, but he cannot *preach*. For to preach a man must know the authority of being under Authority.

Further, he must know something of the authority which derives from service, from being the 'willing slave of all'. When a priest seeks to impose his own authority – 'I am in control of this parish; what I say goes' – then the real authority goes out of the window. When the week has been spent in lowly service to his people – the service of intercession, of visiting, of the menial job gladly undertaken – then the clergyman need not fear that his Sunday ministrations will lack the stamp of genuine authority. 'The Son of man did not come to be served but to serve . . .' (St. Matthew xx, 28).

In fact and in short, there is an authority attaching to personal holiness which can be found nowhere else. It is the *sine qua non* of any ministry worthy of the name. He alone can exercise an authoritative ministry who often has recourse to the secret place of the Most High, who has learned to listen to the God Who speaks, who knows the meaning of obedience, who can say not merely, 'I hold this view', but, 'I am held by this God'. There is something self-authenticating about the authority of a man of whom it can be said by the man in the street as it was said of Elisha by the woman of Shunem: 'I perceive that this is a holy man of God who is continually passing our way' (II Kings iv, 9).

There is nothing brash or noisy about such authority as we have just sought to describe. This is the very reverse of cock-sureness. When Jesus exercised His authoritative ministry, the people were reminded of the words of Isaiah:

> '*He will not strive, He will not shout,*
> *Nor will His voice be heard in the streets.*
> *He will not snap off the broken reed,*

Nor snuff out the smouldering wick . . .'
(St. Matthew xii, 19–20)

So sensitive was His dealing with people, so reverent His handling of personality. There was no forcing of His views, no crushing of individuality. The reed whose usefulness seemed to have been finished might perhaps be coaxed back to uprightness; the wick which only gave out an evil smell might be fanned again into a clean, light-giving flame. Who was to know? It was worth trying. Human nature is a tender thing, and it calls for tender and patient handling. And, judging by the Gospels, the greater the sinner, the more tender was the handling given to him by our Lord.

This tenderness of approach to the individual, this absence of brashness, betokened no lack of sureness of touch. The surgeon who really knows his job, whose experience has taught him the complexities of diagnosis and of the ills that flesh is heir to, once he has made his decision will not hesitate to use the knife. St. John's story of our Lord's dealing with the woman at the well (chapter 4) shows at once the infinite tenderness of His approach and the rapier-like thrust of His charge – 'the man with whom you are now living is not your husband; you told me the truth there' (v: 18). Tenderness and authority can go hand in hand. They did in His case. Nor do such insights into the recesses of human character belong only to the learned. Many a university graduate has been humbled by the shrewdness of the 'unlearned and ignorant'. Such insight is but another illustration of the authority which belongs to holiness.

What has been said above, however, must not lead anyone to retreat behind the cover of a pietistic woolly-mindedness. There is a measure of authority which belongs to the man who is master of his subject. There is an expertise which belongs to the priest's office which has to be worked at and which can only be gained by long and patient study. The preacher, for example, must be an exegete, able by special study and constant application to wrestle with the ancient texts and to indicate their relevance to the people to whom he ministers. Not only is he an exegete; he is a *hermeneut*; and Hermes, be it noted, was the *messenger* of the gods.

C

The only thing which the bishop hands to the deacon and priest at his ordination, and the archbishop to the bishop at his consecration, is a Bible. Perhaps the lack of authority in the ministry of certain men is due to the fact that they have failed to grasp, or have forgotten over the years, the deep significance of that act, and the significance of the reiterated emphasis of the Thirty-Nine Articles on the authority of Scripture. The authority of the creeds rests in the fact that they may be proved by most certain warrant of Holy Scripture' (Article 8). The Church has 'authority in Controversies of Faith', but is itself under the authority of God's Word written (Article 20). Councils may err – 'wherefore things ordained by them as necessary to salvation have neither strength nor authority, unless it may be declared that they be taken out of Holy Scripture' (Article 21).

There is very real authority inherent in the message which we preach. The Christian believes that God has spoken, in a unique way, in the Person of His Son; not only in His teaching and His example, but supremely in His mighty redeeming acts. When St. Paul summarised the essential content of the message which he brought to the Corinthians, nervy in himself but confidently assured about what he preached, he put it in credal form: that 'Christ died for our sins . . . that He was buried . . . that He was raised . . . that He was seen . . .' (I Corinthians xv, 3 ff.).

These are the mighty acts of God, to which nothing can be added, acts wrought out once and for all on the stage of human history. This is the *kerygma*, the thing preached; this is the *paráthéké*, the sacred treasure committed to us. It can only be expressed in a great series of indicative verbs: God loved; God gave; the Word was made flesh; Christ died for our sins; He was raised by the power of God. These indicatives are the very stuff of which the Gospel is made. There is no good news without them. It is only in the light of them that we can ever face the imperatives of Christianity; but when we have grasped, or been grasped by, the indicatives we find the imperatives to be not only possible but a joy to obey. There is authority inherent in the message itself, for it is the very word of God to *homo viator*.

The expertise of the pulpit – for preaching is, *inter alia*, a craft the practice of which calls for steady and life-long application – can only be learned slowly and, it may well be, with a strange mixture of pain and joy. But the more it is learned, the greater will be the measure of the preacher's authority. This, however, is only one – though it is one of the greatest – of the spheres in which a priest's expertise and his authority will go hand in hand. The skill of the administrator, of the chairman, of the sick-visitor, of the pastor, of the counsellor; these and a dozen others as they are learned will add the sureness of touch which leads the onlooker to say: 'This man has the authority of one who knows his job.' In an age such as this, which is the age of the professional, this is not unimportant.

I turn for a moment, though with great diffidence (for I have had a bare thirteen years in the episcopate) to the particular exercise of authority which attaches to the episcopal office. There are occasions when a clergyman says to his bishop, 'I will go to such and such a benefice if you, as my bishop, order me to do so.' I think there are occasions when such an order is called for and must be given. I can only say that in my own experience I have hardly ever given such an order. I believe that, shall we say in ninety-nine cases out of a hundred, it is vastly preferable to follow that principle which we noticed in our Lord's handling of men, and to give direction rather than directions.

Thus anything approaching domineering authority is avoided, and the man who seeks his bishop's advice is helped to grow towards maturity of judgment. Let the bishop think through the problems with the man concerned. Let him ask questions which will help him to get his thinking straight and which will disentangle the primary issues from the secondary. Let him pray with him, or at least assure him of a place in his prayers, and then leave the decision to him.

Is such a course of action the avoidance of the exercise of authority? I think not. It may well be the exercise of authority at its best and most sensitive. Thus Albert H. van den Heuvel can write: 'In order to be able to give authority to any conclusion or event, the recipient must have had some part in its establishment. That is true for parental authority and for intellectual authority, *but also for spiritual authority.*' (*The Humiliation of the Church*, p. 82. The italics are mine).

The question of the right size of dioceses is much under discussion at the moment. It is not wholly unrelated to our theme of authority. The matter has been brought to the fore by Leslie Paul in his *The Deployment and Payment of the Clergy* (1964). There he makes much of the loneliness of the clergy and the need for smaller dioceses than those which we have now in England – dioceses in which the bishop can in truth exercise real pastoral *episcope*, knowing his men and being intimately known by them. There is much to be said for this view, though in fairness it should be added that probably hardly ever before has there been such closeness of contact between the bishop and his clergy as now exists. This is partly due to the ease of modern transport and partly to a new, or perhaps one had rather say revived, grasp of the meaning of episcopacy.

Nevertheless, there is a measure of loneliness among some clergy, as one who has charge of a large diocese, predominantly rural in character, can well judge. Nor is this loneliness only due to a refusal on the part of some clergy to share in the fellowship which chapters, ruri-decanal conferences and so on provide – such men are rare, I am thankful to say. Loneliness is a reality to be reckoned with and its elimination, or at least its amelioration, must be worked at. But is the answer to be found (to put it vulgarly) in the bishop being so close to his clergy that he is constantly breathing down their necks? Is this the best kind of episcopal authority? Is the best pastoral work in the parishes obtained this way? I very much doubt it. Is there not, rather, something to be said for the diocesan bishop at least having a measure of detachment which will enable him to view his intimate diocesan and parochial problems against a wide background and in a broad context? It would be to the loss of the British people if at least some of her diocesan bishops were not national figures.

And the best parish priests, I am convinced, do their best parish work if they are given a large measure of responsibility and are left room for the exercise of a large measure of individuality. It is, of course, of first importance that every clergyman in a diocese should know, from the day of his ordination, that he has the right, at any time and on any matter, to go straight to his bishop for consultation and advice. And it should go without saying that the *first* call on a bishop's time and care should be his clergy, their families and their problems. But given these basic facts, and given the constant movement of the bishop up and down his diocese, it may well be that beneficent episcopal authority cannot always be measured in terms of the smallness of the diocese over which he presides. Now that, in view of recent Church legislation, 'lawful authority' has been more closely defined, it should be possible to exercise pastoral authority without clipping the wings of local priestly responsibility, initiative and individuality.

It is a fact that many of the main issues exercising the minds of churchmen at the present time have in common problems connected with authority. The revision of Canon Law, which has occupied the Convocations and the House of Laity for many years, is basically concerned with authority in the governing of the Church's life. Now that the work is virtually completed, we may ask ourselves whether we have not at times succumbed to the temptation to legislate in detail and to give directions rather than direction. If, in fact, we have done so, our successors will not bless us. It has been a temptation to others than Christians to lay on men's backs legislative burdens grievous to be borne.

The matter of synodical government, which has perplexed the Church for many years and on which, we may hope, we shall soon see some definitive steps taken in England, has at its heart the problem of authority. Where shall this authority be found, in matters doctrinal as well as practical? Is it to be confined, at least in matters of doctrine, to the bishop sitting in synod with his clergy? Or have the laity the right to share with their brethren of the clergy in discussion of and decisions about matters theological and liturgical? The past few years have seen them doing this by courtesy. I am one of those who hope that the day will very shortly arrive when we shall see them doing so as of right. An authority shared among the whole *laos* of God will lead not to the impoverishment but to the enrichment of the Church of God. I take it that the promise of the gift of the Paraclete, of His leading and of His teaching, was made to the whole Church and that the whole Church has the right to go forward leaning on the reliability of that promise.

'By this shall all men know that ye are My disciples, if ye have love one to another' (St. John xiii, 35). It is likely that a future historian of the Church of the first six decades of the twentieth century will have to record that the most remarkable feature of its life has been a growth in love and understanding between different branches of the Church. The century opened with an appalling ignorance existing between the adherents of different traditions. Misunderstanding was rife. Rivalry often took the place of co-operation and asperity the place of a desire to learn and appreciate. But during these decades, and especially since the Edinburgh Conference of 1910, the founding of the World Council of Churches, and the visit of Archbishop Fisher to Pope John, there has grown up a great yearning for actual unity and a measure of loving understanding and of co-operation in evangelism and in Christian philanthropy which could hardly have been dreamed of when the twentieth century dawned. For this we may thank God and take courage as we move steadily forward to further organic union.

Especially we may be thankful that we can detect a growth in the authority with which the Church can speak when the leaders of the main traditions unite to make their voices heard. Disunity results inevitably in lack of authority. How can a world, terribly torn by divisions of race and ideology, be expected to hear the voice of a Church which itself has not found the way to unity? 'Physician heal thyself,' the world may sadly say, and hardly be blamed for saying it. But with the return of unity – a unity based on the twin foundations of love and truth – will come a return of authority. 'By this shall all men know. . . .' 'May they all be one: as Thou, Father, art in Me, and I in Thee, so also may they be in us, *that the world may believe* that Thou didst send Me' (St. John xvii, 21). The need for an authoritative voice, proclaiming the word of God and declaring the will of God, should act as a constant spur to those whose task it is to promote the unity of the Church; and that does not mean only those who attend the great world conferences dedicated to that end!

We have imagined a future historian writing up the tale of

the Church of the first six or seven decades of this century. If he will have to start his story with a substantial section given to the subject of Church unity, it is likely that only second in importance will be the subject of the handing over of authority by the Church of the West to the leaders of the Churches of the emergent nations. No longer does the white missionary go as part of a great and growing Empire structure, the whiteness of his skin suggesting that he may dominate while others serve! Rather, his white skin often constitutes an embarrassment and his national background is a cause of stumbling. He may only remain if he is prepared, in actual fact, to *serve*. So it is that we have watched the handing over by the white races of positions of leadership to men whose faces are dark and, very frequently, whose grandparents knew nothing of Christianity. Authority has passed from West to East.

A glance at the photograph of the Lambeth Conference of 1968 as compared with that of 1958 or 1948 will illustrate this, as will the fact that during the primacy of Archbishop Geoffrey Fisher four different provinces were inaugurated in Africa: West Africa (1951), Central Africa (1955), East Africa (1960) and Uganda (1961). For all the tremblings and forebodings, is not this cause for unfeigned rejoicing? After all, final authority belongs neither to the Church of the West nor of the East, but to the Lord of the Church. 'Full authority in heaven and on earth has been committed to Me. Go forth therefore and make all nations My disciples; baptise . . . and teach them . . .' (St. Matthew xxviii, 18). Such authority as we have is an authority delegated to us by Him and held in trust by us for only as long as He wills.

We began this essay with a reference to the authority which marked the life and teaching of Jesus, and we sought to distinguish between an *authority* in response to which men found – and find – their freedom and life and an *authoritarianism* which cramps and confines. When, on All Saints' Day, 1966, Professor Ian Ramsey was consecrated Bishop of Durham in York Minster, the sermon was preached by the Master of St. John's College, Cambridge, Canon J. S. Boys Smith. I conclude by quoting an extract from that sermon, for, in reverting to that

with which I began, it adds point, as I could not, to the principles which I have tried to outline: 'He taught them,' we are
told, 'as one having authority, and not as their scribes' (St.
Matthew vii, 29). What kind of authority was this? What sort
of following, of obedience, did it, and does it still, demand?
Does it demand that the following be absolute, unconditional,
that we must (if need arise) leave *all* and follow? To that the
answer is Yes. But does that mean that the following of Christ
is to be unquestioning, unsearching? Such a following would
not be the following of *Christ* at all. It would be to miss the very
heart, all the originality and promise of His summons. Had
His call been to a blind following, its authority must long since
have ceased to carry weight.

'His demand was very different – both higher and harder.
He told us that we must have the single eye, that we must *look*,
look with direct, unprejudiced sight, look that we may *see*. You
cannot tell in advance what it will be that, when you look, you
will see; and it is for no man to prescribe it for you. But you
can be sure that, unless you look with the eye that is single, it
will not be the truth that you will see. And remember that, if
no man may prescribe for you what you shall see, still less may
you seek to predetermine it yourself. Your duty, and your
privilege, is to look that you yourself may see.

'This governs and pervades the teaching of Jesus. It is this,
that He Himself had the single eye, single and searching, and
that His call to others was to look as He looked that they might
see as He saw, and in the end it is only this that gave, and still
gives, to His summons and to Himself, an unconditional
authority, an authority that derives from insight and rules by
conviction.'

Sir Bernard Lovell, O.B.E., F.R.S.

Professor of Radio Astronomy, University of Manchester
and Director, the Experimental Station, Jodrell Bank

Many years ago when we were deep in our financial troubles
during the construction of the radio telescope at Jodrell Bank
one of my colleagues said to me jokingly: 'Why don't you issue
a gramophone record with some strange noises on it and claim
that you have received messages from intelligent beings on the
planet Mars? The sales would be immense and our financial
problems at an end!' I remarked that our authority and careers
in scientific research would also be at an end.

This light-hearted conversation epitomises a remarkable
feature of the contemporary world: on the one hand the great
authority of the scientific pronouncement, on the other the
slender thread on which the authority of the individual
investigator may depend. The strength of the authority is such
that, in the face of its pronouncements, the public is sensitive
and gullible. The nature of the authority is such that forces may
be unleashed which condition the world for good or evil. The
consequences of the authority are that governments must
support the activities and developments of the scientific
profession with great sums of money: otherwise they place at
risk the industrial and military strength of their people.

The emergence of authority in science

The basis of scientific authority changed abruptly and dis-
continuously in the seventeenth century. For the whole development of the human race before that period the authority was
that of the sage; generally resting on philosophical or aesthetic
principles. Thus, the basis of Aristotelian astronomy depended
largely on the view that the sun and the planets moved around

42

the earth in circles 'because' the circle is the perfect figure and that the stars were unchanging and embedded in the crystalline sphere of the universe 'because' the sphere is a perfect form.

Within this perfect, geocentric framework astrology flourished as a means of predicting events on earth from the disposition of the stars, sun, moon and planets. During the Greek era the astrological conceptions of causation became a matter of public and national concern wherein, for example, it seemed clear that the constitution and fortune of the individual were determined by the configuration of the stars at the moment of his birth. The world was one in which the occurrence of unusual or irregular phenomena – such as the advent of a comet or a display of meteors – were portentous.

The predictions of astrological 'science' do not survive the test of the experimental method and the basis for this type of authority in science was extinguished over three centuries ago with the development of the Copernican and Keplerian theories and the observations of Galileo and Tycho Brahe. Nevertheless, the enormous power and appeal of astrology are evident today in the survival of some of its features. In more primitive communities, particularly, the belief in 'magic' and esoteric happenings survives. More surprising is the persistence of astrological beliefs in more educated communities, promulgated widely in the supposition that one's prospects might be foretold from the arrangements of the planets in association with the constellation under which one was born. Most surprising is the recent upsurge of the belief in 'flying saucers'. Even amongst the higher intelligences of educated communities one finds a profound belief that 'u.f.o.'s' or 'flying saucers' are in some way supernatural and frequently associated with extra-terrestrial intelligence or visitation. The depth and

43

sincerity of this belief in many individuals are so great that it cannot be shaken even by the immense authority of the contemporary scientific investigator who can find no single piece of real scientific evidence in favour of anything other than natural terrestrial or geophysical phenomena for the 'sightings'.

The authority which science exerts today is the result of the evolution of the scientific method over more than three centuries. Over this period man's knowledge of nature and his physical environment has been cumulative – at least if a broad view of progress is taken. Historically the change in outlook is associated with Galileo. He was not, of course, the first to question the perfectionist doctrines or the ancient schemes of the universe. The cardinal point is that he was the first scientist to base his questioning on observations. In his hands the newly developed telescope revealed the moons of Jupiter and the phases of Venus, making a continuation of the belief in the static earth at the centre of the universe impossible. An *observational* conflict between the beliefs of a scientist and theological doctrine erupted in a most bitter form. The important feature is that the authority of the Church was challenged in a particular and entirely new manner. The challenge could not be met by denial, since the evidence of the challenge was there for any who would wish to observe the phenomenon for themselves.

From that epoch science achieved quite a new significance in the affairs of man in two important respects. As scientists explored the universe and their own immediate environment, the conflict with the authority of the Church developed. It has never been satisfactorily settled and the uneasy situation has continued to erupt in various forms and aspects to our own day. Secondly, with the accumulation of knowledge man became able to alter his environment and his daily life through a technology developed from scientific knowledge.

The first of these issues raises the question of the status of knowledge. It is, of course, a fallacy to believe that scientific knowledge is the only knowledge which is true, and conversely it is equally fallacious to imagine that all scientific knowledge is itself true. Neglect of the first condition leads to an intellect, by no means uncommon, so possessed of the power of the scientific method that it maintains that all problems can eventually be solved. There are many examples of this mode of thought: for instance, the all-embracing issue of the origin of the universe.

The development of the telescope, both optical and radio telescopes, with associated astronomical techniques, has now enabled astronomers to achieve a great knowledge of the universe. Within half a century the known boundaries of time and space have regressed by vast increments; with a rapid succession of new discoveries. Today it is relatively easy to study galaxies and other peculiar objects so far away from our own galactic system that the light and radio waves which we receive from them have been travelling through space for many thousands of millions of years. Since we see them at the time when they *emitted* the light or radio waves, this implies that we see them and study them, not as they exist today, but as they were many thousands of millions of years ago. Thus, as we penetrate into space so we penetrate into time past and can thereby form an opinion of ever earlier states of the universe.

There is a particular feature of the observation of the remote galaxies – the red shift – which leads to the conclusion that the universe is not a static entity but that its constituent parts, namely the galaxies and clusters of galaxies, are receding from each other at high speeds. The derived velocities of recession are significant fractions of the velocity of light, and these recessional velocities increase linearly with the distance of the galaxy. The impression is that the universe is expanding from an original highly condensed state of the primeval material. A knowledge of the relation between the velocity of recession and distance of the galaxies – that is, a knowledge of the slope of the straight line defining this relationship – enables us to estimate that this condensed state may have existed about ten thousand million years ago.

The idea that the universe originated by a 'big bang' from a super-condensate of primeval material ten thousand million years ago has been widely popularised. The point to be emphasised here is that, although the available observations of the the universe appear to be consistent with such a viewpoint there is, in fact, no decisive scientific observation which confirms this theory. Indeed, a deeper study of the appropriate cosmological theories shows us that the available observations, including those of the expansion of the universe, are consistent not only with the big bang idea, but with a whole series of other concepts relating to the early state of the universe. In some of these models the history of the universe may not necessarily have involved a highly condensed condition at any epoch.

The astronomical literature of recent years has been full of claims and counterclaims that some new series of observations provides conclusive evidence in favour of the big bang or some other concept. The ability to penetrate observationally into the past history of the universe clearly carries with it eventually the possibility of arriving at some incontrovertible view regarding the early history of the universe. So much may be conceded but the further claim that, with increasing instrumental powers, it will some day be possible to give a scientific description of the origin of the universe, seems to be quite extravagant and, indeed, shows a lack of awareness of the limitations of the scientific method. In this particular case the difficulty is fundamental and twofold; firstly associated with the finite velocity of light which implies that the epoch of time zero is beyond the observational horizon; secondly because of the basic uncertainty principle in science which, in its simplest form, implies that the very act of observing an event must inevitably influence the event and make our knowledge of it inexact.

In this case, of the history and origin of the universe, we see an example of the possible extent of scientific knowledge and at the same time its limitations are revealed. Science may give us exact information about the early stages in the history of the universe; but the methods of science can do no more than speculate on the origin of the universe. On this occasion the knowledge derived from philosophical and theological enquiry has at the least an equal status and authority with that derived from the scientific approach.

It might be considered that this general principle which maintains that over wide fields of human interest and activity scientific knowledge has no more authoritative status than other forms of knowledge is self-evident. There are, however, many cases of significant importance to human life and thought where the principle is not self-evident. The cosmological issue here described is one example where claims are frequently made concerning the superiority of scientific knowledge. These claims cannot be justified in the deepest sense, and the limitations of the scientific approach must be understood, otherwise the processes of scientific research may lead to claims to authority in realms of activity where other knowledge has an equal or greater status.

If knowledge derived from the scientific approach is not the only knowledge which is true, then what of the converse of the general principle? Is all scientific knowledge true? Although it is tempting to give a categorical assurance that all knowledge derived by correct scientific procedures is true, it is important to realise the limitations of any such assurance. Existing knowledge may not be incorrect but it is frequently merely a part, only, of the true facts which may still have to be revealed. Consider the history of our knowledge of the solar system for example. At various epochs over the last few thousand years man has believed that he had the true and complete facts about the solar system. For thousands of years man believed that the earth was fixed at the centre of the universe. When a scientific instrument (the telescope) became available to test this belief it was found to be untrue. Then Kepler established his laws of planetary motion according to which the earth and the planets move in ellipses with the sun at one of the foci of the ellipse. His prediction of the size of the ellipse in which a given planet moved and its orbital period around the sun could be tested against the measurements of Tycho Brahe. Theory and observation were in accord – after thousands of years of erroneous belief, scientific knowledge, in which observation agreed with theoretical concept, was able to give a true account of the motions of the solar system.

This scientific knowledge of the motion of the earth and the planets around the sun seemed to be true although man's reason revolted against the concept. There was no understanding of why a massive body like the earth could move in space in this manner. What maintained it in motion and why did it not fall into the sun or fly off into space? The genius of Newton provided the answer in the form of the universal law of gravitation that two bodies attract one another with a force proportional to the product of their masses and inversely proportional to the square of their distance apart.

Thus, at least in the case of the solar system, by the mid-eighteenth century man appeared to have true knowledge derived from the scientific approach, about the nature and motion of the system of earth and planets. The planets had been known since ancient times and the overall dynamical system seemed to be closely governed according to the theoretical scheme of Kepler's laws, originally derived empirically and subsequently found to be a natural consequence of Newton's law of gravitation. Then, in 1781, Herschel discovered a seventh major planet – Uranus – the first real observational addition to man's knowledge of the solar system for a few thousand years. Subsequently it was realised that the planet had been observed on at least seventeen occasions in the previous hundred years but had been believed to be a fixed star. As a consequence of these earlier observations it was soon found that the position of the planet did not agree precisely with the theoretical predictions based on Kepler's laws with the necessary allowances for the perturbation caused by the other planets. Furthermore, a few years of observation after Herschel's discovery revealed that Uranus departed from its predicted position by a significant error.

The remarkable story of the independent and simultaneous predictions of J. C. Adams in Cambridge and U. J. J. Le Verrier in Paris that the inconsistencies must be caused by yet another planet further away from the sun than Uranus is a classic in astronomical history. The new planet – Neptune – was discovered by J. G. Galle at the Berlin Observatory in 1846. The story was repeated again less than a century later when in 1930 C. W. Tombaugh at the Lowell Observatory in America discovered the planet Pluto during the course of a systematic search for a trans-Neptunian planet predicted by Percival Lowell and W. H. Pickering on the basis of discrepancies in the motion of Neptune.

Although it was believed that the motion of the planets was entirely explicable on the basis of Newton's law of gravitation there was a phenomenon associated with the motion of the planet Mercury – the advance in the perihelion of the orbit –

which remained unexplained until Einstein's general theory of relativity was applied to the problem. Thus, even in the case of the universal law of gravitation, which seemed firmly established as the basis of the dynamical system of the entire cosmos, it was found to be true but, in fact, a partial truth of a more generalised relationship. Further, today, there are many authorities who believe that the general theory of relativity itself is an approximation, or a part of a more generalised and all-embracing relationship still to be discovered.

The same type of story could be unfolded about our knowledge of the physical condition of the solar system – the gradual realisation even during the last few decades, for example, that the interplanetary medium is neither empty space nor simply constituted, but is a complex of particles and radiation. Similarly with our knowledge of the physical condition of the planets. The initial observation of the planet Venus which led to the view in the early years of the century that it was a luxurious tropical abode of vegetation has had to give way, as a result of the investigations with the modern techniques of the radio telescope and the space probe, to a picture of an arid planet, hostile to vegetative and life forms.

It might be held that this type of discussion is of purely intellectual and theoretical interest, in so far that the implications of truth and the consequent status of authority of the observations and theory have no relevance to the practical affairs of man. This is a superficial and perilous attitude. For example, if the best available measurements of the distances in the solar system had been accepted as completely authoritative, then in 1960 no rocket launched from earth, however perfect its guidance, would have approached within thousands of miles of the planet Venus. Only after the new radar measurements of the distance of the planet had been successfully achieved was it found that all previous measurements and estimates were imprecise. The knowledge then existed of sufficient accuracy and truth to facilitate the successful and important rocket flights to the planet made during recent years.

The status of scientific knowledge, the question of its accuracy, is of paramount importance in the practical affairs of men when we consider the second point concerning the development

D

of technology based on scientific knowledge. It is here that we see in full force the peril of neglect of the consideration of the precision and authoritative status of scientific knowledge.

Today technology and science are intermingled and so confused in the minds of individuals and governments that the efficient development of both is sometimes in jeopardy. The ancient works of man, the great monuments of Stonehenge and the Pyramids, the devices of war, the chariot and the warship, were built by a technology based on elementary principles thousands of years before the emergence of science as a means of gaining cumulative knowledge. Today, technology is based on scientific discoveries which have been cumulative for three and a half centuries, revealing new features of nature and constantly adding to the precision of our knowledge; thereby creating a corpus of authoritative facts on natural phenomena capable of standing the test of repeated investigation. The technological application of this knowledge to human affairs has influenced the civilised world in dramatic fashion. This influence has been irregular and without the all-embracing conscious direction which is necessary for the future security of human civilisation.

Suppose, for example, we consider the influence of scientific technology on the modern counterparts of the works already mentioned. The great monuments and cathedrals have been little affected. All the modern materials and concepts used, for instance, in the rebuilding of Coventry Cathedral, shortened the time scale of construction by not more than a few times over its ancient predecessor. The functional result is the same and the net consequences of the differences between old and new is insignificant in the affairs of man. In the other case, the devices of war, the change to a technology based on science has, manifestly, had dramatic effects.

The most obvious and significant example is the development of the explosive and the means of delivery. Throughout ancient times a chemistry based on alchemy had little influence on the power of the explosive weapon. Then, with the development of chemistry as a science, new explosives were devised. The destructive power of weapons increased enormously even between World Wars I and II, not merely because of the increased explosive efficiency of a given weight of material but also because it became possible to carry and deliver much greater weights to the target areas by means of the aeroplane. However, no one appreciated in the early stages of World War II that the great forces of destruction evolved through a technology based on science could be superseded in an entirely discontinuous manner.

In the years immediately following World War I, Rutherford made the decisive investigations which revealed that the atoms of matter consisted of a dense central, positively charged nucleus surrounded by a number of electrons. Almost simultaneously the development of Einstein's theory of relativity showed that mass and energy must be regarded as equivalent. A decade later the first atoms were transmuted by bombardment artificially; and, at least in principle, man had reached the stage where the difference in mass of the atoms transmuted in this way was realised as energy. The demonstration of the scientific principle was there, but still no man foresaw that new forms of transmutation would soon be discovered in which vast amounts of energy could be released in explosive forms.

The basic discovery of the fission of the heavy elements involving the conversion of a significant mass loss into energy was made in 1939. Under the stimulus of war an unprecedented technological effort was devoted to the transference of the basic scientific principle to produce weapons of destruction immensely more powerful and sinister than any developed from classical chemistry.

The atomic bombs of Hiroshima and Nagasaki were released from aircraft, but already new forms of carriers for explosive weapons had been used in Europe in the form of the V1 and V2 rockets. It is perhaps fortunate for the civilised world that the simultaneous development of the rocket and the atom bomb occurred on opposing sides in this conflict.

Even with the realisation of the atomic bombs of World War II man was using only a small part of the energy contained in the basic uranium or plutonium of the bomb. Shortly afterwards the development of the hydrogen bomb increased the efficiency of the explosive process. In these manifestations of a technology based on science we see a close liaison between the practical application and the scientific fact established at a given moment of history. Throughout the last half-century man's knowledge of the atom has been merely partially true at any given stage. Today the scientific knowledge of the structure of matter and particularly of the atomic nucleus is true only in a restricted sense. There is still no authoritative view of the fundamental structure and forces in the nucleus. Existing knowledge enables man to make inefficient use of the energy contained in matter for power in peace or destruction in war. The efficiencies involved are low – only a fraction of a per cent of the rest mass of the material can be realised in energetic form. Some of the strange objects which we study in the remote parts of the universe are releasing immense quantities of energy and it seems possible that in these objects processes are occurring in which a rather high percentage of the mass is converted into radiative energy. It is possible, and indeed probable that on earth during the next few generations man will uncover even deeper and more fundamental truths about the forces and particles involved in the nucleus. The lesson of the past is that technology will press hard on these fundamental discoveries and for good or ill will make available to man in practical form these deeper and more refined truths of scientific discovery.

The exercise of authority in science

During the last twenty years the cost of scientific research has increased by amounts far in excess of the rate of economic growth in the major powers. While the U.K. has struggled to achieve overall growth rates in the economy in the three to four per cent per annum region, the growth rate in the budget for research has often exceeded ten per cent per annum. Even in the current (1968) phase of devaluation and economic crisis the growth rate for the scientific budget has not been forced below the seven to eight per cent region. In fact, even in phases of acute economic difficulty we find a growth rate for science at least twice that of the most favoured sector in the rest of the economy. Similar features are apparent in the economic development of the major world powers.

In terms of money spent per annum this means that the current scientific budget of the U.K. is between five hundred million and one thousand million pounds. The precise amount spent on basic research as distinct from technological development is difficult to assess. The current budget for the research councils which dispense money from the exchequer for direct support of fundamental research in universities and research institutions is about eighty million pounds covering medical, agricultural, natural environment and the physical, astronomical and space sciences. However, considerable additional sums are directed into these activities through the university grants and the annual budget for fundamental scientific research alone in the U.K. must be today of the order of a hundred and fifty million pounds. Industrial organisations, the defence services, and funds directed into the atomic energy authority and into space and aeronautical technology through the Ministry of Technology account for the remainder. These extremely large sums of money have to be compared with the total scientific budget of about six million pounds per annum for the years immediately preceding World War II.

This remarkable escalation has occurred for a number of complex reasons. First, the evidence of the overriding importance of science in the war effort created a situation where it was impossible to return to the relative pre-war neglect of science. The increasing numbers of people entering the profession then set up a chain reaction of supply and demand, forcing an ever-increasing expenditure on the educational facilities for scientists in the schools and universities. At least, in the beginning, the argument that the economic strength of the country depended on its investment in scientific research was unchallenged. The striving for leadership and parity in the military field led to a colossal concentration of scientific effort in the fields of nuclear science and technology and in aeronautics and astronautics. The evidence of Soviet achievement manifested in the launching of the first Sputnik in October 1957 led to a further dramatic upsurge in scientific endeavour in the United States. The scientific effort in the world has now reached the stage where, according to a recent estimate, something like ninety-nine per cent of all scientists who have ever lived are alive and working today.

The exercise of authority in the domain of scientific research is clearly a problem of the utmost concern and importance in the civilised world. Furthermore, in contrast to many of the other aspects of public finance, a highly specialised knowledge must be involved in the making of decisions. It is therefore important to ask by what processes and by whom is the authority exercised and how decisions are taken to finance particular aspects of research. The essence of this problem is that of bringing responsible and highly professionalised scientific advice to the directive strata of the government of the country. The great powers have tried various solutions of this problem but no satisfactory answer has been found.

The exercise of this authority by an individual or a small group has been held to be the ideal solution. Unfortunately there are a number of profound difficulties in this concept. The main stream of advance in research occurs in the youth of the world. The ideas which lead to the breakthrough and the main bulk of original research are manifested in the age range from about twenty-five to forty. Few people within this group have either the desire or the breadth of outlook over more than a narrow range of scientific effort to qualify for advisory activities outside their own domain. In practice, therefore, the competitors for the authoritative role are found amongst the elder scientists; and they in turn must seek the advice and knowledge of the contemporary scene from their own advisers who are more closely associated with the day to day activities of the younger men. Hence, we find that in any advisory structure a complex system of committees appears to be inevitable. A further fundamental complication arises because of the conflict which always exists amongst the individuals in the higher echelons as regards the advice which should be tendered to those who exercise the final authority of the country.

There are cases where, because of personal affiliation, or for some other reason, a single individual has exerted influence as a strictly personal adviser to the head of the Government. The classic example of this in our own age is the case of Lord Cherwell during the Churchill administration of the Second World War. With the nominal governmental post of Paymaster General, Cherwell acted as Churchill's personal adviser on scientific matters and frequently did so in a dictatorial manner leading to action on the scientific-military front which would have been against the advice of the main body of senior scientific opinion in the country. The personal conflicts and animosities in this story have been well documented by Lord Snow.

There is, too, a reverse danger in this situation where eminent scientists attempt to exert individual influence on the Head of Government. During the years of the Churchill-Cherwell association the realisation of the enormous military potential of the atomic bomb became apparent to a few of the nuclear scientists concerned with the researches into the structure of the atom. In an attempt to persuade Churchill that a great effort should be made to develop these researches with the possibility of producing a bomb of unprecedented power, arrangements were made for Neils Bohr to visit him. Bohr was universally acknowledged to have the respect and confidence of everyone in the world associated with this work, and he visited Churchill when he arrived in this country after his epic escape from Copenhagen in a Mosquito bomber. Unfortunately Churchill reacted unfavourably to Bohr and refused to consider the arguments which Bohr advanced. In Germany, too, it became known after the war that the German scientists had failed to gain the support of Hitler who was more obsessed with the possibilities of his secret weapons – such as the V1 and V2 rockets. On the contrary, in the United States the intervention of Einstein and others with President Roosevelt led to the enormous scientific and technological effort which led to the bombs of Hiroshima and Nagasaki.

We find therefore today that in the major world societies the scientific effort is directed and financed through a complex system of committees and advisers differing in detail but not in essence in such diverse communities as the Soviet Union, the U.K. and the U.S.A. It may be doubted if the freedom of the individual scientist to pursue particular lines of research differs greatly throughout these communities. At the highest levels the decisions can concern only the broad fields of research and, although it might take years to bring it into effect, it is here that national decisions can be taken, for example, to stimulate biological research and reduce nuclear research, by altering the relative financial provisions. Once these decisions are taken the arrangements for the details of the work quickly become the prerogative of the committees of scientists and the individual directors of the scientific laboratories. Only in the U.S.S.R. do the details of this arrangement differ markedly from those of the Western Powers. There the Academy of Sciences has effective control of all the research institutes and the attempts to specify in considerable detail the actual research to be undertaken lead to a most undesirable form of bureaucracy in research. The combination of individual influence and bureaucratic control in the Soviet Union has led on the one hand to the triumph of the Sputnik and on the other to the disastrous episode of Lysenko, whose false genetics could never have survived the free criticism of the corpus of biologists in the U.S.S.R.

These complex and detailed structures exist within the major powers to advise the Government on the expenditure of two to three per cent of the gross national product on research. Although the mechanics of the decision-making may be described, the intellectual content of the processes defies analysis at the present time. Our age, in fact, is typified by the attempts to make statistical analysis of the relevant factors such as cost effectiveness – the effectiveness being variously concerned with such factors as the numbers of students produced and value to the nation's industry and economy. It has been widely believed that a close correlation exists between investment in research and the growth of the national product. This belief seems to have been falsified by a comparison of the various European countries which has shown that the U.K. with the largest growth rate in its science budget has had the lowest economic growth rate. This in turn has led to an analysis of the disposition of the students trained in science and to attempts to direct the investment in research into those subjects which are held to have a greater industrial and economic potential. No one has authoritative answers to these problems.

The underlying feature of the present difficulty in the exercise of an absolute authority in science lies in the extraordinary growth of the subject. Even with expenditures amounting to three per cent of the gross national product it has become impossible either to finance or to educate enough scientists to pursue all the possible avenues of scientific research which have now been opened. Indeed, this feature of growth which makes authoritative overall direction so difficult does itself create a situation of potential danger to man unless the correct decisions can be made. The intense penetration of science into the bio-logical and behaviourist aspects of life creates new dangers beyond the type of development in the physical sciences which has led to the present delicate balance of power in the world. In the free communities the exchange of scientific information is so complete that it is hard to imagine a series of administra-tive decisions which might lead in secrecy to the unbalanced development of aspects of science with new and dangerous mili-tary potentials. Unfortunately, with the present division of the world there can be no certain security against unilateral de-velopments leading to a sudden and serious unbalance of power either in the industrial or military sense.

The processes by which scientific authority is exercised in contemporary society are confused and unsatisfactory. A stan-dard of judgment based on scientific merit is no longer a suffi-cient guide to investment in specific projects or broad avenues of research. The complicating factors of eventual economic benefit, military and human consequences are vital in the equation of judgment. We are rapidly moving into a world where great areas of possible research must remain without investigation simply because the nations of the world cannot finance the effort. The decision regarding the directions of effort in the next decades could turn out to be the most significant in the history of man, and the study of the exercise of authority leading to such decisions is manifestly a matter of the greatest import-ance today.

Individual authority and the emotional conflict

Except in the occasional and unusual cases of the type already mentioned the exercise of authority in science is a collective operation. It is rare for this collective authority to be the un-animous version of the individuals who contribute to the making of the decision. In nearly all cases it must be regarded either as a majority decision or a compromise version. In this respect the scientific field differs scarcely at all from the daily practical and political decisions which have to be made by the governing authorities.

This may seem to be a strange situation in view of the definitive and positive conclusions of the scientific technique. Faced with the need to take a decision about the immediate future of a scientific programme it might be thought that the processes of scientific endeavour would automatically and inevitably lead a group of professionals to an unambiguous and single recommendation. The authority of the individual arises because, as a result of his experimental and observational processes, he is able to predict with a high degree of precision that certain events will occur. For example, the precise dates and times of eclipses of the sun and moon for centuries ahead; or that if one undertakes certain specified procedures with uranium or plutonium then a devastating explosion will result.

However, the individual who can predict in this authoritative manner is unable to pronounce with any similar authority on the consequences of investing a million pounds in scientific research on, say, oceanography or further researches into the atomic nucleus. He can neither predict the outcome of the scientific investigations nor their effect on the practical affairs of men. Furthermore, it is found with a surprising degree of frequency that the really important discoveries in a programme of scientific research arise as an accidental by-product of the intended investigation. For example, in our own age the discovery that the long wavelength emission in the radio wave part of the spectrum was reaching earth from outer space was made accidentally by Karl Jansky in 1931 when he was working on a problem in radio communications for the Bell Telephone Laboratories in New Jersey. This chance observation led, in a generation, to the development of an entirely new science of radio astronomy, absorbing significant amounts of the scientific budget of the nations and having close technical affiliations with space research and optical astronomy. The development of that subject itself has been full of further accidental discoveries in its short history; for example, the quasars in 1960, and in 1968 the discovery of the pulsating radio emitters during the course of an experiment to investigate a quite different phenomenon.

Hence the individual, however great his authority based on previous success in scientific research, cannot necessarily claim a definitive measure of authority as far as future decisions are concerned. It is, of course, often claimed that the training and mode of thought of the professional scientist do give him the authority to guide the future developments. It seems clear, however, that practical experience shows that this claim cannot be justified and that a large measure of emotional judgment enters into the problem. If it were not so then there would be near unanimity amongst the professional scientists when faced with the problem of decision-making affecting their own science.

The general problem of the impossibility of financing all possible avenues of research opening up before us today has been discussed already. It is a problem of increasing urgency that the governing bodies of the nations should be able to obtain decisive advice from the body of their scientific advisers. This advice is, of course, constantly given but there are few cases where it is either decisive or unanimous. The oceanographer, the nuclear scientist, the biologist, the astronomer and the space scientist will all wish to proceed with their own subject. Since no nation can now afford to finance all these individual researches to the limit someone, somewhere, has to decide whether to spend a million pounds on developing oceanography or to use it for further developments in nuclear science or any of the other subjects. The individual at the higher level of consultation, although he may be in that position because of his wide experience, nevertheless inevitably has an emotional connection with his own subject and his colleagues working in that speciality. In this way the processes of the exercise of collective authority become intermingled and entangled with the emotional judgment of the individual.

The emotional content in authority is exacerbated by a new feature of scientific research. The growth of the scientific budget has been largely a consequence of the enormous sums of money which have to be spent today on individual projects or at least on specific disciplines. Nuclear research and space research are big science in the sense that the machines or facilities for the research cost many millions of pounds. Furthermore, even when the capital expenditure is completed it is found that the annual budget for the support of such facilities must be maintained at a comparable level with the annual capital outlay during construction. We have today, therefore, almost reached a watershed in which, within the feasible overall budget for science, it is difficult to embark on expensive new projects unless some existing ones are closed down or reduced in scale. It is here that the individual judgment based on scientific assessment is entangled in its severest form with the emotional and other vested interests of maintaining that which already exists. Indeed, since the effective authority in science must be the consensus of the attitudes of the individual there is real danger that the efficiency of progress in scientific research will be seriously impeded because of the retention of vast projects which have already served their purpose. These monopolise the manpower and finance which on a rational and unemotional scientific judgment might be better employed in developing other lines of research.

Apart from this conflict within science itself, there is also a developing emotional and practical conflict with the social environment. On the one hand, the individual whose authority contributes to the corporate decision is a member of the community, sharing its pleasures, facilities and dangers. With increasing effect voices are raised in the great powers that the money spent on big science would be better employed in dealing with the social problems which beset the community. So far it has been possible to dismiss this attitude because the scientific budget has been so low. However, for reasons already discussed it seems likely that the world powers have either already reached, or will soon attain, an effective ceiling where the scientific effort absorbs a fair and reasonable proportion of the economy and where it is also limited by the manpower which can be trained effectively in its disciplines. It must now be conceded that this issue can no longer be dismissed as we reach the saturation phase of scientific endeavour.

This aspect of the conflict is well illustrated by the space research activities of the U.S.S.R. and the U.S.A. The urgent need for new houses for the people of the U.S.S.R. is self-evident and yet, according to an official U.S. source, the annual budget of the U.S.S.R. space programme equals the annual expenditure on new housing in that country. In the U.S.A. the advent of the Sputnik stimulated the vast effort to catch up and beat the U.S.S.R. in this new technological field. 'Space is a new ocean on which we must sail. Let us harness the rich resources of this nation to place an American on the moon in this decade,' said President Kennedy shortly after his election. Within a few years the budget of the National Aeronautics and Space Administration climbed to six thousand million dollars. Now, only a few years later, Congress is forcing significant reductions on this budget and the leader-writer of the *New York Times*, who was clamouring for this American effort in 1961, expresses a widespread feeling about the decreasing tendency of the space budget. 'Now that the desired space research capability has been created, it is merely good sense to shift some of the resources thus employed to other and more urgent national needs. Individual scientists or engineers may regard space problems as more glamorous than such tasks as cleaning up the nation's polluted air and water, providing high speed land transportation or working out faster and cheaper ways to build new housing to replace the noxious and overcrowded slums. But can there be any doubt that these and related terrestrial needs are more important for the time being than work on landing men on Mars?'

As long as the amounts of money and men available for research were insufficient to occupy the possible scientific manpower it was easy to dismiss such pleas. Today a new situation is developing where the authority of the individual scientist cannot be contained within a restricted framework of a single research item. The decisions on the disposition and direction of the available scientific manpower and money are of a paramount importance to the survival and vigour of the world communities.

High Master, Manchester Grammar School, 1945–62
Vice-Chancellor, University of York, 1962–

Education is one of the means by which a society both imparts to its immature members an accepted body of knowledge and transmits to them certain patterns of behaviour. Hence the extent and justification of the authority of the educator is a subject of particular importance. It clearly has two major aspects. The first concerns individual educational institutions. Who should wield the authority within them? How strong should this authority be? What kind of questions should it decide? The second aspect of the problem concerns the responsibility of educational institutions to the community, including in that general term the whole machinery of the State. It clearly includes a variety of questions ranging from such personal ones as the right of parents to choose a particular school to the justification of some agencies of government to determine the balance of studies in, say, a university. Both of these aspects of the central question of the role of authority in education raise problems of great interest and importance, and on many of them there exists a considerable degree of disagreement. Certainly, in a short essay of this kind it will not be possible to consider them all, still less to attempt their solution. This is particularly true at a time like the present when all the relationships we shall be discussing are far more fluid then they have ever been.

This is shown very clearly if we consider first the most obvious of educational relationships, that between the teacher and the pupil in the school. Two centuries ago it was possible for a great and good man, John Wesley, to write of education: 'Break the will; whatever pain it costs, break the will, if you

62

would not damn the child.' It is a phrase which if used today in an essay would be almost sufficient to ensure the failure of any student in a college of education. In the centuries since Wesley wrote, and particularly in the past fifty years, the whole tone of relationships within the school has completely changed. The factors leading to that change have been complex. The most fundamental could be traced by one with the knowledge and space at his disposal to such profound stirring of ideas within western society as was shown by the Reformation, the revolutions of the eighteenth century and the Romantic movement, all of which in different ways emphasised the importance of the individual personality and judgment at the expense of established codes and, although the process took time, the emphasis on the individual has spread downward from the adult to the child.

More directly, the influence of Dewey and still more of his many followers, many of whom have misunderstood and thereby exaggerated his actual position, has been profound. It has been one of the factors which have made possible the emergence of individual teachers who have carried libertarianism to extreme lengths, some of them men of strong personality and, in their own situations, remarkable talents, such as A. S. Neill. It must be said straight away that the new atmosphere in the schools has been in many ways entirely beneficial. Schools of nearly every kind are much happier places than they were half a century ago. Fear has often given place to respect and cooperation; rote learning to an attitude of discovery of new knowledge; concern for the needs of the individual child has replaced an attitude (never, of course, by any means universal) of treating children simply as members of a class.

Yet we must be aware of the dangers of excessive libertarian-

63

ism. Its philosophical foundations are, to be charitable, extremely dubious. A writer like Neill will condemn the aims of a 'conventional' education to create certain codes and attitudes in a child and regards such a 'moulding' process as a violation of the spiritual autonomy of the individual. Yet his method of allowing virtually unimpeded freedom is overtly directed towards the production of 'better' people. The removal of any restraints, even if it is right, rests on a view of what is desirable in a human being, and the attempt to realise it by creating a certain kind of environment is as definite and 'moulding' as the most authoritarian régime. The merits of such a teacher must not blind us to his shortcomings as a philosopher or as an example.

Even if the collective authority of the pupils is invoked, e.g. by the use of school councils and the like for dealing with disciplinary problems, can we be anything but sceptical of the results, although if properly used they can be a useful apprenticeship in the exercise of authority? They can be dangerous because the young are apt to be more intolerant and more cruel than their elders. Reformers must not forget that it was during their worst days of brutality at the beginning of the nineteenth century that the boarding schools relied most on the pupils looking after themselves, since in some no adult was in evidence between six in the evening and six the following day. Nor is it safe to base moral authority, as is implicitly done by the excessive libertarians, on the 'good of the community'. Some of the greatest crimes (e.g. the extermination of the Jews in Germany) have been perpetrated with precisely this justification.

It must also be remembered that the child demands security above almost anything else. And security includes a definite and comprehensible moral code. As any adult who finds himself in a position of authority knows, nothing is more exhausting than to be faced every day with a succession of choices, often moral ones. To lay this burden on the young is an abrogation of responsibility that can become deeply harmful. Thus an excessive libertarianism can bewilder and over-burden the child and replace the authority of the teacher by that of the herd, which may be more capricious and more conformist, and is certainly less knowledgeable and experienced. This is one of the points,

among many, which are made with the greatest insight by
Reismen in that remarkable book *The Lonely Crowd*. We must
never forget that the two greatest moral teachers, Jesus and
Socrates, were both considered heretics by their society. An
educational system cannot produce such creative heretics, but
it can do its best not to stifle them, and it may well be that a
nominal libertarianism that recognises no authority but the
will of the majority may be more crushingly conformist than
the individual teacher, for few groups are more conformist than
those to be found among the young.

If the corroding effect of a lack of a proper authority can be
seen among the pupils, it can also be seen in a different way
among those who teach them. The teacher today easily tends
to be so indoctrinated with the fear of indoctrinating his pupils
that his teaching easily loses all force and conviction. Today
too many teachers are so anxious not to appear 'square' that
they commit the ultimate treason of the clerks and confuse
tolerance with indifference. They give the pupils the idea that
if they do not actually share their transitory judgments and
their choice of the easy third rate that takes the place of a hard
struggle to recognise and enjoy the first rate, they are not convinced enough of their judgments to proclaim them. They wish
to run with the hare of student popularity and hunt with the
hounds of hard thinking and a belief in excellence.

Instead of the intellectual and moral leadership that the
young have a right to expect from their abler and more experienced teachers, they leave those they are supposed to educate
in a wasteland of grey neutrality, in which one view seems as
good as another, and where there is no indication of the illumi-
nation to be gained only by rigorous and demanding disciplines.
In much talk of 'students' rights' there is, perhaps, this one,
which is the most important right of all, and which is rarely
mentioned. Too often if one asks a young teacher what the aim
of education should be, he will echo the accepted doctrine that
finds some justification in the Declaration of Human Rights: it
is to enable an individual to develop his personality to the full.
'What, *all* sides of his personality?' one asks. 'Of course, yes,'
comes the parrot answer. Yet when one points out that the
most perfunctory self-examination shows that there are sides of

E

all our personalities that should not be developed, the naïve response comes back, 'Oh, *of course*, we mean the *good* sides', and the responsibility for the teacher that lies behind the word 'good' in this context remains uncomprehended or ignored.

If we reject an excessive libertarianism in our schools, in spite of the undoubted benefits that an atmosphere of freedom has brought, what are we to put in its place? The first line of authority must be the individual teacher. Actually, of course, much more important is the home and probably the social environment, but at this point I am considering primarily education as carried on in overtly educational institutions. The greatest obstacle to discussing the problems of authority in education arises from the kind of black and white dichotomy between the two extremes. It is almost impossible to try to discuss the difficulties of an extreme libertarian position without being branded as an extreme authoritarian. In attempting to assess the role of the teacher who believes it is part of his duty to help his pupils to make value judgments in whatever field, it is essential that we should not simply regard him as a purely authoritarian figure. There is no inconsistency between having firm convictions and yet trying to maintain the most sympathetic and humble understanding of the difficulties of all men – most of all the young. One of the most vital parts of that new approach to the education of teachers for which we all hope, and which is already in some places beginning to emerge, lies in this area of helping those who are in difficulty in evolving a nexus of value judgments on which to run their lives, and an awareness of when to call in those more expert in human problems. One of the first steps in such a training must be to distinguish between the important and the trivial areas in which authority should be exercised. If authority is to be respected it must not be concerned mainly, if at all, with such matters as hair-style or clothing. Distasteful as long side whiskers may be to many of us, it is as well to remember that Dr. Arnold did not find them inconsistent with a strong moral sensibility. In other words, the teacher must decide, and the process of decision is not always easy, what are the really important issues on which guidance, and, in the last resort, authority, must be exercised.

To put a trivial matter in a larger context, authority must always be reasonable, and not only based on reason, but be seen to be based on reason. The ultimate aim of discipline in a school as in a community is not only to make life tolerable for other people: it is to educate individuals to make decisions, and to show them the kind of considerations that should weigh with them in making them. At a time of great fluidity in judgments, particularly moral ones, this can be a very difficult process. It is made much more difficult by the fact that our pupils come from homes which are far more permissive than they have ever been and, much more importantly, by the early maturity of the boys and girls that we teach. The contemporary housemaster who bans *The Catcher in the Rye* from the library forgets that some of his pupils may well have read *Last Exit to Brooklyn* in their homes. Both this earlier maturity and, much more important, a rational approach to the problems of authority make it necessary for us to ask 'Why?' of every rule before the pupils ask it first. If no time has been more difficult for the teacher than our own, none has been more intellectually and morally stimulating in the sense that today we must find rational answers to difficult questions instead of relying simply on tradition.

Ultimately the question of the proper limits of authority in education come back to the formula of the Education Act of 1944. Just as academic education must be adapted to the age, ability and aptitude of the child, so must education in value judgments, including moral judgments. The young child who, as I have said, needs a firm background of rules to protect him from the too heavy responsibilities of choice, must be told what can be tolerated. If John pulls Mary's hair we must stop him, though we may differ as to whether the best means are gentle persuasion, a clout on the head or, if he persists, a psychiatric examination. But stop him we must and, in general, no permanent damage is done to his free development as a personality by so doing. In the same way the child from the home that is insecure in some way, whether through fecklessness, lack of affection or breakdown, is helped by an authority that does not necessarily make his moral decisions for him, but which is intelligent enough to provide a moral framework of considerable stability. With the boy or girl of fifteen or over the problem is different. Then authority must be prepared to argue with the greatest frankness and be equipped to justify its decisions. But it must not be tempted to acquire the easy popularity of being 'with it' by a pretence of sharing the attitudes or conclusions of the immature.

This rational approach to the problems of the older boy or girl is made much more difficult by some factors in the prevailing social climate. Firstly, the very widespread decline in religious belief has removed one of the most obvious sanctions for moral behaviour. In my own view the danger is not simply that we are forced back on philosophical justifications which may be too sophisticated for most of our pupils, or purely social ones which may be dangerous if they involve the idea that value judgments are simply matters for majority decisions. The very close identification between moral behaviour and religious belief, the inadequate remnants of which remain in the 1944 Act, means that the rejection of religious belief may all too easily lead to the position that moral standards will be rejected at the same time. If a child is taught that the only reason for good behaviour is a framework of doctrine which he afterwards finds incredible, as very many do, he may believe himself to be in an amoral world. It is, moreover, a world in which greater affluence (at any rate for many young people), an affluence which has led to whole industries being devoted to its exploitation, the greater general permissiveness of which I have spoken, and a growth in means of communication which makes him more vulnerable while giving him an illusory feeling of sophistication, has led to an elevation of knowingness over knowledge.

The difficulties in the way of finding credible sources of authority for the young are formidable. We can attempt to overcome them in several ways. The first requirement in my view is that the teacher must at all times show that for him questions of value judgment are supremely *important*, whether they be in aesthetics or morals. He may base this belief on a religious faith, but this may be impossible for him. Teachers may, and will, differ over important issues and sometimes this may lead to bewilderment. In the modern world it is inevitable.

But the communication of a belief that there are ideals and rules that do matter is an essential part of a teacher's function.

Secondly, the teacher must equip himself as well as he may to defend his judgments, for example by pointing to the effect on others of courses of action; by pointing out that to live at all requires various acts of faith, and that faith in the value of individual men and women has inspired the lives of people who, by a consensus of those who have studied most deeply the history of human societies, have been good. Thirdly, the young must be given opportunities for actually *doing* things which it would be perverse to regard as other than good, and to harness their strong sense of individual freedom to actual causes. If very often the young seem to their elders to be rebels without a cause, it is perhaps the fault of those elders for not giving them a cause worthy of their energies, or expressing our disapproval of their support for great causes because we do not agree with them. To summarise in a few lines what I have been trying to say about authority in education at this level, its nature must be adapted to the individual, it must be rational, it must be based on knowledge, and it must never be arbitrary or sycophantic.

These problems become more acute as we consider the transition from the school to higher education, and we can take the universities as examples. Here we enter a field which today is presenting particular difficulties in identifying the proper source and limits of authority. It is difficult in the first place to get the matter in proportion and to remember that the majority of students are ordinary, hard-working and often very well-mannered young adults. It is difficult for those of us who grew up in a tradition when it seemed such a glorious privilege to have won one's way to a university that, although rules might be broken, they were never really questioned, to understand at all the anarchic and almost pathological rejection of authority that characterises some students today. Because they are in such a minority it is easy to dismiss the situation as unimportant and indeed I do think that some of the press and TV give too great a prominence to student unrest and have thereby done much harm. Nevertheless, we have now a quite serious situation that has developed very rapidly in the past three or four years. Although we are clearly still very far indeed from the state of most continental and some American universities, we have reached a position in which a group of students, albeit a small group, can make it an occasion for violence if a speaker is invited with whose views they disagree; can, at worst, disrupt the work of an institution altogether and, at best, create a general atmosphere of tension. And perhaps one of the worst effects of all this has still to show itself, for I am sure it will become increasingly difficult to induce men of distinction to work in universities or to leave institutions concentrating on research for a life of university teaching.

Our response is made more difficult, too, by the fact that those who 'represent' the students represent only (and that often precariously) a fairly small minority. The majority of students are simply not interested enough in the running of a university to be present even at the meetings of their represent- ative bodies. They wish simply to pursue their work, their careers, their games or societies, or their love affairs. Our difficulties are increased by the marked tendency of students (like many of us) to want it both ways. They may reject a phrase like 'pastoral care', they may point out that they are adults, and must be left free to run their own lives as if they were young workers, although at the same time they are often reluctant to accept rules which they would find enforced in any boarding house, or a good hotel, and still more in a club, where the idea of playing a transistor after 11.00 p.m., or indeed at any time, would be unthinkable. Yet at the same time these young people *do* complain (and in my view sometimes with justice) if they feel they do not have sufficient contact with teaching staff or far more free psychiatric support than the Health Service provides. Faced with this contradiction, author- ity can be forgiven if at times peevishness breaks through a desirable and, indeed, essential tolerance.

I say 'essential tolerance', for I do believe that if we are to re-create a stable and civilised atmosphere in our universities, we must make a great effort to diagnose the causes of our present discontents, and make what efforts we can to remedy them. What are those causes?

The first is of negligible importance. It is the sheer hooligan-ism that the young tend to show when rather tight or in a mob. It has always been with us, whether in its aristocratic forms, and it was, I think, Evelyn Waugh who described the Bullingdon Club as giving out 'the sound of the upper classes baying for broken glass', or in the young tough on the terraces at Everton. This has little to do with our present discontents, though it may exacerbate them.

Secondly, our student body tends to be more heterogeneous than it was. Quite obviously a greater number come from homes without the same traditions of education and stability as in previous generations, though I think it is very easy to over-estimate this element in the situation. Nevertheless, it is true that before the present wider opportunities to enter a university a greater proportion of the scholars had to win their way from a home which, though it might be financially limited, was one where industry and ambition, not only of a material kind, went hand in hand with a strong moral drive. I think that much more significant than any change in the social composition of our universities, however, is a greater permissiveness in homes of all kinds and in society itself, and a lack of genuine regard for learning on the part of the young. Further, words like *'in loco parentis'* clearly have no meaning when applied to a fairly mature student who may well be married. This diversity among the students is one reason why authority in a university must try to be as flexible as possible and, in fairness to university teachers and administrators, it is often the students who are most anxious that the rules of discipline and appeal should be more clearly codified, and be made more rigid, and these are demands to which one should accede even though it is often the students who suffer, because one can understand their anxiety to avoid the injustices that sometimes follow an exercise of personal authority.

The third strand in the canvas is much more important. It is political, not in the sense that it is closely connected with great issues of national or international politics, but in that it rests on a demand on the part of students to take a much greater share in the government of the university at every level. The students who want this are not those who reject the whole idea of authority or the existence of a bureaucracy: they embrace them. Their demand is to be part of them. The preoccupation of universities with autonomy has led in some of them to a proliferation of committees so luxuriant that one is reminded of a tropical jungle. The idea that the Vice-Chancellor or anyone else has supreme authority is completely misguided. It is upon those committees that students wish to be 'represented'. Three problems at once present themselves. First, do they really grasp the difference between representatives and delegates? Secondly, while it is reasonable that they should wish to be concerned with such matters as catering, of obvious concern to students, what qualifications have transitory and inexperienced individuals, merely because they are students, to sit on the governing bodies of institutions whose turnover may be several millions a year, and whose proceedings may be highly confidential?

Thirdly, is sitting on committees really what a person of eighteen comes to the university for? He will have enough of this, surely, in later life. Our university career is the last time that most of us will ever have of being irresponsible in the best sense, i.e. having no obligation to do anything but read books we presumably want to read, or why come? – of hearing scholars talk, sometimes badly, sometimes brilliantly, about their subjects; of playing games, or making music, or acting in plays, or engaging (as many do) in some form of social service, or simply talking, without the routine of the office or the responsibilities of a family or an institution on their shoulders. Yet these precious years they wish to dissipate in what everyone of experience knows to be the dullest part of administration; not personal contacts, not being part of a major body to produce some significant report, but the routine committee on which their presence is too short-lived to exert any effect, even if they possessed the background knowledge and the experience to accomplish changes of policy.

There are thus in my view weighty arguments why students are wasting their time in seeking for a premature and inappropriate authority. Yet the fact remains that they *do* want it and, even if they are misguided, I think we must go to the limit of what our consciences will allow in giving it to them. I refer to our consciences for we must have some proper regard for such values as efficiency, for confidentiality, and, most important of all, for not creating systems in which students have a say in making decisions from which some academic staff are excluded.

The point at which the students' demand for participation becomes most questionable is where it touches on such subjects as curricula, examinations and even appointment of staff. First it should be stated quite categorically here, though the same principle applies in other fields, that no student need go to a particular university. If we choose him, he also chooses us. If he does not like what we provide let him go elsewhere. Secondly, it is, I believe, legitimate and often valuable that student opinion should be heard on such matters as content of courses or method of teaching. But it is very doubtful whether formal student representation on committees is the best way of dealing with this, for the ablest students are usually unwilling to be concerned with administration and prefer to educate themselves. In any case, it is very difficult for a student to say what should be included in, say, a chemistry course until he has nearly completed it, for until then he scarcely knows what it comprises. We are in danger, too, of a movement towards facile generalisations about social relevance and soft options. In fact, as in so much else, the most valuable interchanges are those between teacher and taught at a personal level, which presupposes something like a tutorial system, and a university that is not so large that decisions are too remote from the student-teacher situation.

The fourth element in student protest is the most worthy. It is the reaction of a genuine, thoughtful and informed idealism towards what the students consider the evils and injustices of the world, whether they be Viet Nam or racial prejudice. It is a reaction confined neither to students nor to this generation. I saw it at its best when I was privileged to visit South Africa at the invitation of the students of the English-speaking university of Witwatersrand. There, and in Cape Town, faced with a denial of reason and humanity, a great body of students make a brave and continuing protest, the more impressive because it is completely orderly, attractive to the most gifted students, having the full support of the majority of academic staff, and carrying on side by side with its protests constructive work of personal service towards those whom it seeks to help. If our young people did not feel deeply enough about such great moral issues to express their views on them, then one might despair. But if such non-violent protest is unavailing, what then? And the only answer one can give is to say that where the very thing against which one protests is the power of brute strength over moral conviction and intellectual argument, then by adopting the methods of one's opponents one is oneself corrupted. It is this kind of protest, informed, moral and above all based on rational argument, that universities partly exist to make.

Lastly, there is another element which is at the heart of violent student protest as we see it today. It is the most difficult for the universities to meet because it is irrational; the most difficult to analyse because it is ideologically incoherent. It can be confused with the hooligan, the student politician, or the genuine idealist, for it borrows their watchwords and their techniques. In so far as it has a philosophy it is anarchist, though its adherents quote Mao or Marcuse. Whether, as some believe, the whole 'extreme' student movement is infiltrated by small Communist groups, who hope to take power from a state of disorder, it is difficult to know in the absence of hard evidence. The general atmosphere of this fourth element, however, is a vaguely based desire to destroy authority because all authority is corrupt. It is a direct negation of the idea of a university, which recognises the authority of knowledge. Although a minority movement, it claims to represent the many in revolt against the power-élite. Partly such an attitude arises from the general libertarianism of our time. But it is poles apart from some of the classic figures of that libertarian movement. The old rules are discarded: there are none to take its place. This is a non-conformist revolution which destroys all previous authorities and proclaims no successor.

The intellectual and moral situation is made more confused by the new material environment in which we live. The scale of opportunities and the complexity of the modern world make the machinery of decision more technical and more remote from the individual man and woman. Thus there is a disillusionment with politics that is only accentuated by the 'inside' revelations of the press. Whereas forty years ago it was possible to feel, without being absurdly simple-minded, that if one worked for the Labour Party and the League of Nations Union then poverty and even war might disappear. Today the 'progressive' young forget the enormous social progress of the years since then and, as for war, they see their own government launching Polaris submarines, or failing to denounce a war that is to them exceptionally cruel and apparently exceptionally pointless. What, some of them ask, can they *do*?

> *'I a stranger and afraid*
> *In a world I never made'*

expresses the feelings of many, particularly those who are temperamentally unstable, or not strongly moved by the subjects they are nominally studying.

Some of those who protest are intelligent. They are certainly sufficiently intelligent to know that the whole strength of their movement with its microphones and pamphlets rests on a technology they affect to despise. At a deeper level they know that to create the 'social justice' or the educational opportunity, let alone the greater amenities, which they demand as a right, presupposes a growth of administration and control in society which they simultaneously reject.

There is an inner contradiction in their position which increases their frustrations. They are faced, at the worst, with a world which is in some ways more precarious, more depersonalised, more mechanised, and which to many seems more incomprehensible than ever before. It is a world at once too complex to understand and too impersonal to control. It is symbolised in most countries far more than in Britain by universities that have become so large that they appear to be vast factories, and by mass methods of teaching which are the reverse of that discussion in small groups which is a vital element in true education. It is increased, too, by the emphasis on research rather than teaching that characterises many contemporary universities.

Faced with these frustrations, the young respond in several ways. In a good university where they are conscious that their seniors care about teaching them, and even educating and helping them, and where they realise that even the 'establishment' cares about some of the causes that disturb them, the majority concern themselves with the task of preparing themselves for a life which may involve changing the world, but which will base action on knowledge. But to an increasing minority this is too sluggish a response. Towards politics they adopt a facile cynicism, a complete indifference, or a violent distrust, since an impotent democracy has become a cover for the machinations of 'they'. Alternatively, they can try to withdraw from a wider social life and its responsibilities altogether, through drugs, or a bogus mysticism, or through an intense cultivation of personal relationships. They can, and sometimes do, end in mental breakdown, or they may demonstrate, often violently, against any or all authority, either because they themselves want power or because they believe that authority has created a world that contains so much pain and corruption, forgetting that many of those in authority have devoted their lives to fight the same evils.

To many of us all these manifestations are profoundly depressing, particularly in universities, not because we are illiberal, but precisely because all our presuppositions are liberal ones. Because we have believed with Mill that freedom of discussion among educated people will ultimately move towards truth, that the best approach to general well-being is through humane legislation and administrative action, we are discouraged and alarmed by much that we see and hear. We have held, and still hold, that some experiences are more valuable than others, and have fought for an education that shall enable ever more people to enjoy them, and we are in danger of disillusionment by the growth of a movement which denies a whole set of attitudes – attitudes of which universities should be the highest expression.

Intellectually, we can show that this denial is illogical; that the anti-university will teach them nothing; that the unorganised society is impossible, or not worth living in, and that the highest achievements of the human spirit in art or music or literature or science have always been achieved by those working within a framework of rules, often a very rigid framework. We can claim that the taming of technology so that it becomes our servant and the means to a truly better life, and not the creator of a world of material satisfaction, alienated from the life of the mind and the imagination, demands increasing and disciplined intellectual endeavour. We can admit, and indeed proclaim, that it is one of the supreme tasks of higher education to encourage a critical attitude in those we teach. Should we then resent it, if that relentless questioning of presuppositions is directed towards ourselves, or our own institutions? Of course we must not. But in adopting this civilised approach to education we must not lose our nerve, or betray our principles. We must continue to maintain that criticism is justified provided, and only provided, that it is directed towards subjects important enough for an educated man's attention; that it is expressed in rational ways, in argument worthy of intelligent people and not in words daubed on walls.

I used the phrase, 'keep our nerve' but by this I do not mean adopting attitudes of unyielding opposition or recalcitrant authoritarianism. I mean something quite different. As I have said we must continue to explore every way in which legitimate student participation in every aspect of university life can be encouraged. But I mean more than that. It is true that many of our institutions, our curricula and practices are in need of re-examination and our ideals in need of restatement, though to be fair those processes are going on far more vigorously than many of our critics imagine. We must devise and encourage methods of organisation and teaching such that even in large institutions no charge of impersonality or inhumanity can be brought against us. But these processes must not only go on, they must be *seen* to go on, so that the hard, small core of those who are unwilling to accept rational argument or clear evidence shall be recognised and discredited for what they are.

Thus, though willing to change, to experiment, to discuss, we must not be frightened or coerced into adopting practices or attitudes that we believe to be wrong or irrational, or sacrificing standards of learning to meet superficial inter-pretations of 'relevance'. Even the old have a right to principles. And the principles of free discussion, of grappling with difficult and original ideas, of reverence for the liberal intelligence, of affirming that the unexamined life is not worth living are those for which at their best the universities must stand, and must refuse to allow them to be distorted or destroyed. If we do, then we shall indeed betray the students themselves, by debasing the very things we exist to give them.

We have hitherto been discussing the sources and limits of authority within educational institutions. We must now turn to a different series of problems that arise when we consider the relationship between those institutions and the community in which they exist. Who in the last resort ought to control the schools and universities? Who should decide what goes on within them, and who should be admitted to them? These are clearly matters of great importance. It must be said straight away that these questions are so difficult and controversial that it is impossible to give perfectly clear answers to most of them. Education is one of the principal means by which a society seeks to perpetuate its values: it is through education that it produces workers of various kinds on which its prosperity, its happiness and, most importantly, the tone and quality of its life depend. It is partly through its education that it will seek to modify or preserve its social structure. On all these grounds the community, principally through the power of the State in one or other of its manifestations, must assume some authority for every part of the educational system, and all civilised states do so. The difficulties arise when we come to consider the limits of that authority. Two factors are tending to widen those limits. One is the growth of egalitarian sentiments, which are part of democratic and authoritarian traditions alike, which assert that the only way to give equality of educational opportunity is through drastic State control. This tendency is now reinforced strongly by economic forces. The quantity and quality of the educational provision demanded by the modern community are making financial demands which the State alone can provide. It is inevitable that the community will demand ever increasing control over the education which it subsidises. We have recently had an example of this process as regards the universities. In England their finances have been scrutinised only by the University Grants Committee. Such an arrangement was tolerated while the amount of State aid to them was trivial. But that support has now become so massive that the pressure for a closer examination by Parliament has become irresistible and it has now been decided, against the weight of academic opinion, although in my own view rightly, that their accounts should be open to the Comptroller and Auditor General and hence to the Public Accounts Committee.

But if one strand of democratic sentiment leads inevitably to regarding the sovereign people as the proper ultimate authority for the control of education, another fears this intrusion of the State into activities that must be primarily concerned with the mind and the spirit. It was this fear that led some nineteenth century thinkers, for example Spencer and J. S. Mill, to oppose State education altogether, and which leads many of those who emphasise the libertarian rather than the egalitarian aspects of democracy to favour the continued existence of private educational institutions, at any rate in competition with those controlled by the State. Here we have one of those not infrequent examples of the way in which holders of beliefs about authority that spring from common democratic sources may be led to completely contrary conclusions. The necessity for compromise that usually follows is the source both of the strengths and weaknesses of any anti-authoritarian society. Thus, although we all agree that the State should enforce the compulsory education of all children for at any rate ten years, and that it should have the power to ensure the maintenance of certain minimum standards, both in its own interest and to protect the individual, the necessity to compromise has led to the bewildering variety of educational systems with which we are familiar. In England, educational institutions range in independence from completely private schools to others completely administered by Local Educational Authorities, a transition that includes schools partly controlled by religious denominations, and others directly under central government, while universities guard jealously an autonomy that has been only very marginally eroded by the fact that the greater part of their income comes from the State in one way or another.

In the conditions of the modern world it is inevitable that more and more educational power should pass to the State, almost certainly in the form of the central government. I should say frankly that this does not fill me with the alarm felt by some of my friends. For sixteen years I was head of a school financed by central government. No greater freedom than I possessed would have been proper even if, indeed, it had been conceivable. But such a happy state of affairs is possible only if certain conditions are observed. If our interpretation of a democratic educational system means increasing control over educational institutions, we must examine with the greatest care what the limits are to the power that the layman should wield over the practitioner. The layman, whether he be an elected representative or other, represents the needs and aspirations of the community which in any case supplies the money. Some control he must have. Yet if he attempts to prescribe, say, the content or the methods of teaching he will not only be speaking from ignorance and, therefore, often be wrong, but his interference will enervate or frustrate the professional whose work is involved.

The authority of the expert provides one of the most interesting problems for a democracy, whether he be a civil servant, scientist, or other professional. It is one that we must solve if we are to be efficient enough to survive. And in no area is it more difficult than in education. This difficulty arises partly from the fact that this is a field in which nearly everyone regards himself as knowledgeable. Men who would hesitate to express views on nuclear physics, or mediaeval French, or selling shoes speak with confidence and definition about education. And to some extent this is healthy, for it recognises that education is a wider matter than what goes on in schools. And, indeed, the term 'expert' is a most ambiguous one when used in educational contexts. In my own view, we are in danger of giving too much authority to the educationist and too little to the teacher. But, whatever the difficulties, I believe that if our educational system is to be at once more democratic and more efficient, we must put more rather than less faith in the experts, whether they be civil servants, teachers or administrators, and reserve to the majority of laymen control only over the widest and most general matters.

Whitehead summed up the position when he wrote: 'For example, in the teaching profession it is obvious that young students cannot be subjected to the vagaries of individual teachers. In this sense, the claim for the freedom of teaching is nonsense. But the general community is very incompetent to determine either the subject matter to be taught or the permissible divergences to be allowed, or the individual competence. There can be only one appeal and this is to general professional opinion as exhibited in the practice of accredited institutions.'

Of all academic institutions it is universities that are most jealous of their autonomy and to whom the greatest degree of self-government by those who work in them is accorded by common consent. It is actually not self-evident why this should be so. Such a degree of self-government is unknown in other kinds of educational institutions, although the Weaver Report has taken a great step forward as regards the Colleges of Education. It is interesting, however, to hear a university teacher, who one knows would strongly resist an extension of the power of laymen in university affairs, expressing the most authoritarian views as regards the government of schools. The emphasis on the autonomy of corporations of teachers and scholars, moreover, has its dangers, as we have seen, if the 'scholars' begin to take their part in it seriously. Finally, one is sometimes alarmed lest the passion of university communities for 'self-government' may not lead to such a proliferation of committees that a number of the staff may simply not have time to fulfil their obligations to teaching and scholarship and where 'democratic' processes of arriving at decisions will lead to a loss of any coherent idealism or sense of direction. As Mark Pattison wrote of nineteenth century Oxford: 'The men of middle age seem, after they reach thirty-five or forty, to be struck with an intellectual palsy and betake themselves, no longer to port, but to the frippery work of attending boards and negotiating some phantom of legislation, with all the importance of a cabinet council – *belli simulacra cientes*. Then they give each other dinners where they assemble again with the comfortable assurance that they have earned their evening relaxation by the fatigues of the morning's committee. These are the leading men of our university, and who give the tone to it – a tone as of a lively municipal borough; all the objects of science and learning, for which a university exists, being put out of sight by the consideration of the material means of endowing them.'

The real justification for making universities as free as they

F

are can only be the ability of those who work in them and, although it is one that I myself would accept, it has Platonic overtones that put in this direct form would not really commend it to many of those most devoted to university freedom. It is, however, a healthy thing for society that it should show its recognition of intellectual pre-eminence by the degree of freedom which it gives to the institutions which should embody it.

If it is inevitable that universities should be regarded as the supreme examples of what we regard as citadels of academic liberties, it is less clear what we regard these proper liberties to be, which must be defended at all costs. The liberty to think, to talk, to publish what we believe to be true, to follow the argument where it leads, is one that is susceptible only to minor limitations without irreparable loss, and society will encroach upon it at its peril. The liberty to choose one's own students, though often claimed and to some extent justified, is dangerous. Were the universities justified in the nineteenth century in excluding half the population (i.e. women) from entrance to them? Are the universities of South Africa justified in excluding students whose colour is other than pinkish-grey, though in the greatest of them it is the will of the State rather than that of the universities that, to their eternal credit, enforces this irrationality? The position as regards academic autonomy as I see it is this. Of course it is inevitable that universities should be responsive to some social pressures because of the money that pours into them from public and private sources. It is not only inevitable but right, for nothing could be more harmful than for a university to give the impression of an ivory tower that values only dead or socially irrelevant knowledge. But, as I have said, the idea of usefulness held by the university is not, and should not be, the same as that held by society at large. The function of universities is not simply to respond to social needs but to transform them; not simply to give the community what it wants, but what it ought to want. For at their best, places of higher education are, in the modern world, a world where religion has lost its universal authority, the chief custodians and interpreters of value in society. If this role is to be dynamic and not merely conservative, as it has often been in the past, the university must be free; free to choose its curricula and its staff, free above all to encourage its members to follow the argument wherever it leads and thereby to discover new knowledge, and free to think new, and sometimes dangerous, thoughts. These are the vital freedoms. But if they are to be preserved in the face of greater financial dependency, greater publicity and the influx of many more students from uneducated backgrounds, the universities must exercise their liberties responsibly. Their relations with government must be co-operative and not suspicious; their expenditures must have regard to reasonable economy; their attitudes be clearly affected by social concern. But behind these obligations lie greater ones. They have an obligation to culture, to interpret what Arnold called the best that has been thought and written; the obligation to add to knowledge; the obligation to engage in social action; and lastly the greatest of all, to open the world of the mind and the spirit as widely as possible to the individual student. To pursue these aims, to reconcile them where they conflict, should be the aim of the university.

I have referred to the universities' function of not merely giving the community what it wants but what it ought to want. Thus the universities are themselves a source of authority in society. The danger of a democracy is that it will accept the will, not of elected representatives, but of a mob, even in judgments of value; that it will commit the error for which Pilate has been vilified through the centuries. It is the duty of universities at their best not simply to pursue truth, for some truths are so trivial as to be valueless, but rather to establish a hierarchy of values in their own proper sphere, the domain of the life of the mind. It is their function to assert the authority of rational thought and dispassionate investigation, to sustain the allegiance which a civilised society owes to a great tradition of culture on the one hand and to the exploration of new truths on the other. It is only on their success in discharging this function that the ultimate justification for such autonomy and authority as the universities, and the individuals in them, may demand can ultimately rest.

Formerly Permanent Secretary,
the Ministry of Housing and Local Government

There are two facets to the authority of a civil servant, as of anyone else engaged in business. One is his authority in relation to the outside world; the other his authority within his organisation. The first is of the greater public interest and I propose here to confine myself to this.

The authority of a civil servant is limited; indeed it might almost be said to be non-existent. In the *Oxford English Dictionary* the first definition of the word 'authority' is the 'power or right to enforce obedience; moral or legal supremacy; the right to command or enforce obedience'. In this sense, the civil servant has, in general, no authority at all. With rare exceptions, specifically authorised by Parliament, the civil servant has no power or right, in his own name, to enforce obedience; no supremacy; no right to give an ultimate decision. He can act only in the name of his Minister; every decision given is the Minister's decision; for every decision the Minister is answerable – in the courts as to its legality, in Parliament as to its propriety. Nor can the Minister delegate his authority. He cannot evade his responsibility.

But to many people the assertion that the civil servant has no authority will sound like the grossest hypocrisy. For who is it who really takes the decisions? Indeed, to what extent can ministers, birds of passage as they so often are, reach their own decisions? How often does one read or hear that it is the Civil Service that 'runs the country'? When I retired from the Civil Service more than one person said to me: 'Won't you miss the *power*?' And when I answered, truly, that I was not conscious of having had power, except in relation to the organisation of

Civil Administration

---

the department, this was seen, I am afraid, as just part of the hypocrisy. There is a widespread belief that the authority of ministers is, largely, a sham. I am sure that it is not; but I think there is some danger that it is sliding that way.

Everyone knows that the great majority of decisions made in the name of a minister are, in fact, made by civil servants without reference to him. A minister cannot himself see more than a fraction of the cases, amounting perhaps to many thousands a year, which he is nominally responsible for deciding. Time and again he will find himself defending decisions of which he was unaware until they were challenged – sometimes even decisions with which he might not have agreed. A Parliamentary question, an article in the press, a letter from a Member of Parliament, perhaps a chance word in the corridors of the House of Commons, may be the first he knows of what he has decided; perhaps even the first he knows of the extent of his responsibilities in the particular field. It is a very hard thing to be a minister – far harder than the public have any notion of. But that is by the way.

This doctrine of ministerial responsibility has come under a growing strain as the scope of government has extended – which it has done enormously since the end of World War I and seems likely to continue doing; and as the decisions of government have cut ever more deeply into private interests. Well aware that ministers can make relatively few decisions in person, and never allowed to know which decisions were taken personally by the minister since that would make nonsense of the doctrine, the public increasingly feel that, whatever the theory, it is the civil servant – unknown, unchallengeable, working in secret – who is in fact exercising the authority.

This feeling constitutes a threat to the whole authority of

government. Submission to authority depends on acceptance of it; and acceptance in a free society where government rests on consent depends ultimately on people being satisfied that the authority has been properly bestowed and is being properly exercised. This means that people want to know how and where authority is exercised – want to have it in the open. But the huge complexity of government today makes this extraordinarily difficult to achieve. It is a problem of government to which I will return. First, however, it is important to understand just how the relationship of ministers and civil servants and the doctrine of ministerial responsibility work in practice.

Departments differ in their kind of work and, to some extent, in their traditions. My own experience has been almost entirely in the Ministry of Housing and Local Government and its predecessors, with some years in the Treasury (the establishment half of the Treasury) during the war. The Ministry in my time has been concerned mainly with the physical environment – the conditions in which people live; with public health, housing, planning. Since all of these are the responsibility of local authorities, a great deal of the Ministry's work consists in dealings with local authorities and with people who object to what local authorities want to do. Inevitably this colours my ideas of how government works. Civil servants whose experience has been with economic affairs, collection of the revenue, technological developments or defence, and so on, might write this rather differently. But essentially the relationship between ministers and civil servants and the mores of the civil servant are everywhere the same.

In considering this relationship one must first remember in what the authority of a minister consists. It derives from law. He can enforce decisions, exercise supremacy, give an ultimate decision only as Parliament has authorised him to do. All his actions are open to review by the courts. This is ground into every civil servant. The first question he asks himself, consciously or unconsciously, on any case that comes to him is: what is the law? Sometimes, indeed, he is irritatingly pernickety about this, to the aggravation of ministers anxious for action, seeing a legal skeleton in every cupboard. Nevertheless, since the authority of the minister derives only from law it is right that this should be the first question, and sometimes it settles the case.

But increasingly over the past half century Parliament has given to ministers a wide discretion to take decisions according to their concept of the 'public interest'. For all that a distinguished lawyer once called such provisions 'Henry VIII powers' and recalled the Star Chamber, this has been inevitable. It is here that the difficulties arise. The authority thus given to ministers is very great. The decisions they reach, or that officials reach in their name, depend not on an interpretation of the law but on policies – on the Government's view of what the public interest requires. So the official who gets a case for decision must make up his mind how the policies apply to it; that is, in effect, what the Minister would decide if the case came to him. If the official is in doubt he must refer the case up for a second opinion.

Many cases are settled at a middle level in the administrative executive hierarchy; most of the rest can be settled by Assistant Secretaries – the heads of divisions. At that level officials should be sufficiently conversant with current policies and sufficiently aware of the attitudes of the Minister of the day to reach the decision with the aid of professional, including legal, advice. But any case that raises new issues, or seems likely to prove very controversial, or is of a kind on which the Minister is known to hold strong views – or, maybe, suggests that the governing policy ought to be reconsidered – will go higher; a good proportion (much increased in recent years) to a minister; one of the Parliamentary Secretaries or the Minister himself. It is part of the training of every administrative and executive civil servant to recognise the case that must go up; but, of course, mistakes are made. Obviously it is more than difficult in a big department for every officer to know how the Minister – the politician – would judge a case; and sometimes the most harmless-looking case contains a charge of dynamite. Always the civil servant is torn, in different degrees according to his temperament, between desire to get cases settled and anxiety to get them right (i.e. what the Minister would think right). Inevitably there is an awful lot of paper passing, which is the outsider's criticism of the Civil Service, or one of them. For the matter of that it is one of the writer's criticisms too.

Always the civil servant is conscious that the authority is the Minister's, not his. He will never try to ignore this, or dodge it, imposing his own 'authority'. What he *will* try to do is to persuade the Minister to his way of thinking about what should (or should not) be done; and as he is permanent his inclination is likely to be against any sharp change of course. He will, naturally, accept the policies of the Government as they may have been expressed in ministerial decisions or speeches or in election manifestos – or, as it seems to him, they are implicit in the Government's general attitudes. He will have his ideas about what the policies should be, given those attitudes; and certainly his ideas about how they could be best implemented. He will know through his years of experience the practical limits to the assumption and exercise of authority by government; to some ministers it will sometimes seem that he has the difficulty to every solution. But his governing idea is to serve his Minister and to find the practical solution to whatever the Minister wants to achieve. A strong Minister who knows what he wants and understands the limits of his authority in practical terms (what his fellow ministers will accept; what Parliament will accept; what the public will accept; what is administratively possible) can get whatever he wants out of his department. Leadership in a government department, as anywhere else, produces an instant response. Any department – only look back in history – is as good or as bad as its Minister. With all its difficulties, even now despite the apparent unreality, the doctrine of ministerial responsibility is, in essence, valid. But if it ceases to be credible, and it is wearing that way, its validity will progressively diminish.

The real authority of the civil service is of a kind which comes later in the *Oxford English Dictionary* definition: 'power to influence the conduct and action of others'. But by what right does he exercise this authority? Later in the definition we read that an authority is an 'expert in any question'. That, I think, is the key. The power to influence others should depend, in part at least, on one's expert knowledge; and so it does if the others are shrewd enough. It is sometimes suggested, especially by people concerned about the current confusion and failure of affairs in Britain, that civil servants exercise far too great an influence over the actions and conduct of ministers while at the same time being too little expert in the questions they have to handle. In short, by virtue of their entrenched position they exercise an authority to which not all of them at any rate are well entitled.

There is something in this. There is a certain amateurishness about the British Civil Service inherited from the Victorian – the Liberal – ideal of the administrator, when government was very much less interventionist than it is today. The permanent Civil Service has virtues which are taken for granted but which are nonetheless immensely important; the virtues of steadiness, incorruptibility, unswerving allegiance to the processes of constitutional government. It has also a high degree of intelligence. But nowadays it needs as well a high degree of expert knowledge in a wide range of very diverse subjects: from the administration of complex social benefits to the ordering of astronomically expensive aircraft; from the management of the economy to the development of an up-to-date educational system, and so on. It is right – for the matter of that it is inescapable – that ministers should be influenced by civil servants. But it is vital that civil servants should have a good title to exercise the influence; should be expert as well as incorruptible, which is not an easy combination. Whether they always have that title is, essentially, the question being examined by the committee on the Civil Service now sitting under the chairmanship of Lord Fulton. Its report will be out before this book is published and considerable changes in the recruitment, training, management and organisation of the Service may result.*

In his handling of cases, the civil servant is always seeking equity. This, too, is ground into him. It does not spring from natural virtue so much as from a deeply seated anxiety to keep the Minister out of trouble. But in the result it is a virtue although a price is paid, often enough, in indecision and delay. The discretionary powers of government are almost never exercised arbitrarily, in the sense of capriciously, or at least never consciously so. One cannot claim this absolutely since any huge organisation contains its quota of stupid, wilful or

* Since this was written the Report has been published as Cmnd 3638.

just impatient people; but equity, which is (the *Oxford English Dictionary* again) 'even-handed dealing', is certainly one of the fixed principles of government administration, very difficult though it often is to apply in practice.

It is a fact, however, that the equity of decisions becomes more and more difficult to discern in some fields of administration, when the private interest must give way to what is deemed to be the public; and this is one reason why the authority of government is being increasingly questioned. A very interesting recent development has been the establishment of the Parliamentary Commissioner, popularly known as the 'Ombudsman', whose function is to examine allegations of maladministration made to him through Members of Parliament; but this is a strictly limited jurisdiction and does not go to the root of equity. More to the point is the discussion going on, though not as yet much noticed, whether some system of administrative law should not be developed in Britain under which the courts would be enabled to review the equity of administrative decisions and perhaps provide remedies to redress inequity wherever it was found.

Observing the ever-spreading tentacles of government, some people suspect the civil servant of a lust for power. But this is true only in the sense that the civil servant is concerned to sustain the authority of government. The constant extension of the powers of government is a response to public demand; and often the civil servant fears it – will try to resist it. His political masters, however, live by votes and it is, in general, the electors who demand increasing government intervention: to provide additional benefits, to control activities which some dislike, to secure a more comfortable life. It is the civil servant who says that if government does this, that or the other, innumerable safeguards will be needed, endless provisos required, administrative machinery will have to be set up; not because he wants to enlarge the administrative apparatus but always with the idea that only so will the exercise of the authority prove acceptable. No doubt he is often too cautious or apprehensive, but such is his guiding motive. In the end, of course, the whole operation may become so laborious and so unintelligible that that in itself makes it unacceptable. Civil servants almost certainly tend to think too much in terms of past attitudes and old dogmas and are frequently wrong in their ideas of what will be acceptable. An experienced minister will often understand the limits of acceptability better than his civil servants, haunted as they are by memories. But the argument is valuable; for essentially it is concerned with the consent of the governed.

Intelligibility is terribly important in securing the consent of the governed – the acceptance of authority; and here government too often fails, though not as a rule for want of trying. Who has not gaped, in near despair, at the forms he is expected to fill up; who has not groaned and given up in the face of some section in an Act; who really understands his rights and obligations? It is perhaps unavoidable that in a highly complex, tightly packed, technologically dominated society the rules that govern the behaviour of the individual should often need interpretation by experts. But intelligibility is not sufficiently regarded; and here the civil servant is very guilty, with his legalistic reluctance to call a spade a spade and his curious jargon which is born partly of his non-authority and is a by-product of ministerial responsibility.

All I can say in defence of my profession is that many of its members are bitterly conscious of this inherent failing and try hard to correct it. They have indeed succeeded in doing a good deal to improve it, though not as yet anything like enough. Ministers make enormous efforts to explain new legislation to the public; in speeches, in fireside chats, in whitepapers, in pamphlets. In part it is the struggle for equity – for even-handed dealing – which complicates law to the point of unintelligibility. But what, I think, is not sufficiently regarded is that some ideas, clear and attractive to the logician, are just too difficult for the ordinary man to comprehend and that, if so, they are probably bad ideas for government to adopt.

So far I have been thinking about civil servants and the philosophy within which they work. It is time to turn to ministers who are the more important half of the equation since it is they who exercise authority. How do they make their policies known to the hundreds of their staff who are administering them? How can they feel sure that what is being done in their name is what they want done? Are they helplessly the prisoners

of their civil servants? How far do they really exercise the
authority which is nominally theirs?

Again it is a problem, at least partly, of communication.
The civil servant must see that the key decisions are brought
to the Minister. He must never be guilty (the temptation can
be very great) of keeping back a case because he fears the
decision he may get. In practice he doesn't: his loyalty can be
relied on. He may not always judge rightly: when he fails he
must rely on the Minister's forbearance. Government will
practically never admit to a mistake; a practice which, I
believe, is taken unnecessarily far. The House of Commons will
usually respect a minister who says: 'I am sorry. I was wrong',
always provided he doesn't do it too often. But many decisions
are irreversible, having the force of law. Apart from that
ministers must as a general rule support the decisions taken;
otherwise the system could not work at all.

The Minister, is not, of course dependent on what is served
up to him to know what is going on. He has a stream of correspondence from Members of Parliament, endless parliamentary
questions on every conceivable subject, Parliamentary Secretaries to keep him aware of feeling in the House, numerous
organisations, authorities, people who get at him directly.
He goes about the country (or the world) a great deal and he
reads the newspapers voraciously.

The most senior staff act as link men between the Minister
and the department. They are, or should be, in frequent contact
with him and can, or should be able to, see that his decisions,
views, attitudes, interests, and phobias are understood by the
staff below. Equally they should see that the department's
problems and ideas are known to him. Acting as link man is
indeed the main job of any Permanent Secretary, together with
his responsibility for the organisation of the department.
Personal contact between the Minister and as many of the staff
as possible is, I believe, invaluable. It does not always happen.
In a big department it is obviously difficult to achieve. But it is
important not only that the Minister should get the feel of the
department and should know whatever varying opinions there
may be, but also that he should keep personal contact with
the staff in the interests of staff morale.

The success of the relationship depends on mutual confidence: confidence by the Minister both in the loyalty and in the intelligence of the staff; confidence by the staff that they understand what he wants to do and will support them if they act in good faith and intelligently. This mutual confidence is almost always achieved in time, although necessarily it takes time where the parties are strangers. Of course, there are clashes; and each party can, on occasion, become thoroughly irritated with the other. But they are engaged in a joint exercise and pursuing a common purpose; whether it be to provide better housing, better education, a healthier economy, a more stable world condition or whatever. And a partnership develops, founded on mutual respect and cemented by shared anxieties.

One of the major problems of modern government is the burden on ministers. If anything goes wrong in the affairs of society – and a great deal does – it is 'they' who are to blame. But which among the critics would take the job on? Ministers work all hours. In addition to their work inside their departments (and they are lucky if they can devote half the working day to this) they must attend meetings of Cabinet and Cabinet committees. Having probably had to study the papers in the small hours they then have to take part in the discussion of issues that are sometimes of appalling difficulty and sometimes trivial – such is the working of democracy. They must spend hours in the House; fantastic hours if they are piloting through a Bill. They must spend time in their constituencies. They must, or at any rate they do, attend innumerable tedious lunches and dinners where, as likely as not, they have to make a speech. They are expected as, perhaps, rulers have been since the world began to be public entertainers as well as legislators and governors. They must spend many hours listening to the grievances, complaints, requests of countless people who too often are quite oblivious of what government can do. 'How small of all that human hearts endure, the part that Kings or Lords can cause or cure.' So said Dr. Johnson; and perhaps every government department should have this in bold letters over the front door for every inrushing deputation to ponder.

In addition to all this one has to remember that ministers are apt to change their jobs with disconcerting frequency. So, often, a minister may start with very little knowledge of the work for which he is responsible. He may have specialised in foreign or in Commonwealth affairs, or in agriculture, or in the problems of exporters, only to find himself grappling with housing, planning, rating. Then is it not inevitable that he must rely on his civil servants to tell him what to do? And do not the civil servants, given these conditions, have it all their own way? Do they not persuade the Minister to do what *they* want and blind him with their greater knowledge of the law and of the government machine? There are two things to be said about this.

In the first place the Minister may be a tyro in the subject matter of his department; though if he is strong and determined he won't be one for long. But he is an expert in politics. He has, normally, had long experience of public affairs in general and of the House of Commons in particular. He has usually been a constituency member for, at least, some years and knows something – perhaps a great deal – of people's problems and difficulties, of the impact which government makes, of the gaps in social provision. He is a representative. If he is a good minister he has, or very soon develops, a pretty good idea of the sort of thing he wants to do; and with experience he also gets a pretty good idea of the sort of thing he can do. A famous story is told of Ernest Bevin when he was Minister of Labour. He wanted the department to prepare legislation to regulate the conditions of employees in the catering industry. Since the industry comprises an enormous range of establishments and the widest variety of working conditions, the department thought this nearly impossible, or so the story goes. After much argument they presented the Minister with a long list of the questions that had to be answered before legislation could be framed. Mr. Bevin took the questions away and brooded over them. Then he summoned the staff and handed back the questions. 'I reckon,' he said, 'that the so-and-so's who are clever enough to ask these questions are clever enough to answer them. We will have the Bill.' And they did.

The other thing to be said is that, as already described, the civil servant's job is to give the minister what he wants. This is the meaning of being a civil servant. It is true that he may have his own ideas of what that ought to be and his own ideas of what, in any case, is possible. But once the minister has, after hearing what is said, made up his mind what he wants then the civil servant will get on with it and will do so whole-heartedly. Sometimes he will encounter insurmountable obstacles but he will do his best to get round them. The policy becomes his policy; he becomes, sometimes dangerously, more royalist than the king.

This, perhaps, is the point at which to consider the real power of ministers and the extent of their authority. If civil servants are suspected of a lust for power, how much more so are ministers, although with less resentment since they are in the open and exposed to fire. Why else should they take on a job so arduous and so risky? Any minister can lose his job at the drop of a hat. But I do not think it is the exercise of power which fascinates ministers, although the hope of it may lure aspirants to the job. For any minister finds himself maddeningly limited in what he can do. Not only is he, as I said, bound by law - and changing the law is an appallingly laborious process - he is also limited by finance. He can never do a fraction of what he wants to do because of this. In short, he is limited by the extent to which we, the public, will allow him to act on our behalf. Further, he is one of a team: he must carry his colleagues with him on any major issue. And he is answerable to Parliament. It is usual nowadays to talk of Parliament as being virtually helpless before the power of the Executive; but in fact it still exercises, in the name of all of us, an enormous restraint over what ministers can do, not least from a government's own back benches. Ultimate authority lies with Parliament and at any time Parliament can exercise it. That it very seldom overtly does so does not mean that the power is not there; and changes are under discussion which would enable Parliament to be better informed and so to exercise its ultimate authority more effectively. For the minister, life is one long series of frustrations shot with all too rare successes.

The burden on ministers is, of course, absurd. Who should sympathise with them? It is thoroughly inefficient. Why don't ministers do something about it? They have only themselves to blame and it is we who are the victims. So runs the criticism.

It is hard for any government to reform its procedures. It is nearly always in the middle of intense difficulties and so far as it can lift its eyes from these at all it can hardly be expected to look much beyond the next election. The pressure for reform must come partly from the Civil Service and partly from outside; from everyone who cares about the authority of government and believes that it could and should be more intelligently and sensitively exercised, as indeed it could and should. Here, too, changes are under discussion; but any radical reforms will need a tremendous heave from informed public opinion to get them through. One of the changes being discussed would devolve some, perhaps in the long run much, of the decision-making to people or organisations for which ministers would have only a general responsibility. One example is a current proposal that responsibility for decisions on the majority of planning appeals, at present an intolerable burden on the Minister of Housing and Local Government, should be devolved by authority of Parliament to the individual inspectors who hear the parties, thus producing the result that people would see who exercises the authority and would have direct access to him. This device, or something like it, might be extended into several fields, so relieving ministers of part of their loads and helping to re-establish the reality of ministerial responsibility.

A bigger and perhaps even more difficult question now coming into discussion is the working of the Cabinet system. Lord Robens has suggested that government should be run much more like a big company, with the principal ministers largely free of paper work and able to concentrate on the major issues. It is not at all easy to see how this could work within a system of parliamentary democracy; but the central idea, that ministers should be freer to concentrate on the big questions they have to resolve, is immensely important. To be acceptable, government must be seen to be reasonably efficient; although one must never forget that the art of government is far and away the hardest that there is. Too little mercy is extended to those who have taken on the hideously difficult job of government; but, no doubt, it is healthy that this should be so.

What does it all come to – this question of authority in relation to government? The Civil Service, after all, is only a part of government. Authority must, in any society claiming to be free, be willingly accepted. To be willingly accepted it must be intelligible: people must be able to understand both the reasons for what is being done and the way in which it is being done. They must also feel assured that the authority being exercised is the authority they have conferred. They need to know who, in fact, is exercising the authority and by what authority. The exercise of authority by 'faceless men' is not, in the end, acceptable. In the British system of government it is ministers who exercise authority. These are answerable both in the courts and in Parliament for what they do or what is done in their name, and so ultimately to the electorate. This is still the truth; but with the enormous increase in the scope of government it is becoming increasingly difficult to discern. The result is that many people are becoming more and more resentful of the authority of government. Yet it is we, the electorate, who have willed the increasing scope. Our real resentment is against the way in which the authority is being exercised. Perhaps government is trying to do more than can reasonably be done. The certain thing is that the methods of government need considerable change if the authority of government is to continue to be acceptable.

The heartening thing today is that we are looking criticially at all our government institutions, recognising the failings and accepting the need for radical improvement. This is something about which everyone who takes an interest in government, and that includes everyone who is critical of it, should feel concerned. For in the end it will be only if enough of us care enough that changes will be made.

G

Lord Stow Hill, Q.C.

Solicitor-General, 1945–51
Attorney-General, April-October, 1951
Home Secretary, 1964–5. Lord Privy Seal, 1965–6

I hope I shall not be thought too lawyer-like if at the outset I try to define to myself precisely what is the question posed to me by the title to which I am asked to write: 'Authority and the Law'. The law consists of a code of rules set out, in this country, in the terms of written statutes or in judgments recorded on decided cases. But what, in this context, is 'authority'? The noun 'authority' is used in many senses. Sometimes, in a legal context, it is used to denote those very 'judgments' themselves – 'are there any authorities on this point?' This is language often used by lawyers to ask whether there exist any recorded judgments which may be quoted to resolve a doubtful point of law. Or lawyers say, 'the opinion of such and such a judge, as expressed by him in a recorded judgment of his, affords authority for a particular proposition of law'. Or, again, there are expressions such as, 'by what authority do you do this or that?'

In other contexts the word 'authority' may be used to denote of an individual a quality of his personality or will power, or superior learning, status or experience which he possesses, apt to enable him to exercise a predominating influence over others and to bend their will to his. And there are many other senses in which the word is used. But, as I apprehend, none of these is relevant to the title, 'Authority and the Law'. By 'authority' in this title I understand something much more elusive to be intended. It is supposed that in society as a whole, whatever is ment by 'society' – perhaps it would be better to say in large, more or less definable groupings of human beings, living together in more or less organised communities whether on a

The Law

national, tribal, continental or other recognisable basis – there resides something that may be regarded as their collective will. 'Society' as a whole in this sense, it is thought, strongly approves or as strongly resents certain types of behaviour and collectively wills that its members shall or shall not behave in the ways approved or resented, as the case may be. In the present context I understand that it is this collective will of society that is intended to be denoted by the term 'authority'. Primitive society often seeks to enforce this collective will by mob rule or the use of force by the stronger. But, in a more sophisticated, civilised society, mob rule and unruly force are replaced by the rule of law.

Nevertheless, because we are human and do not take easily to disembodied 'wills' divorced from living beings who are motivated by them, perhaps, in our thinking in this context, we still grope towards some personalised concept of 'authority'. The image of it that occurs in our minds is, perhaps, that of the whole apparatus of government, Parliament and its members, the press, the courts, the Church, schools, universities, the radio and television; the whole aggregate of individuals who for one reason or another are so placed that they can speak, and be heard or read, and thereby influence the behaviour of the broad mass of their fellow citizens – the recognised organs of society which constitute the repositories of power and influence, all of them goaded, egged on, chided, prodded and checked by an active, restive, noisy public opinion – but all of them (and this is what builds them into a personalised 'authority') lumbering towards and trying to catch the spirit and meaning of and give expression and effect to this elusive collective will of society. To the extent that our image of authority is personalised it is the image of all those persons who are the mouthpieces and exponents of this collective will, namely the whole host of those to whom I have referred. They are 'authority' because they seek to express and enforce this collective will, seeking to impose itself on the rest of us. The question that is then posed is: to what extent is the law an apt instrument to enforce this collective will and, to the extent that it is inept, where are its imperfections for this purpose to be found? It is in this general sense that I understand the question put to me.

First, can the law give expression to this collective will? Is there any difficulty in framing in words the dictates of this will? We often hear in Parliament about the difficulties of finding an appropriate definition. Difficult it often is; but, in my experience, it is very rarely, if ever, that this difficulty cannot be overcome if those concerned – ministers, their advisers and parliamentary counsel – really mean to overcome it. The written word of the law can be made to say almost anything, whatever Parliament really wants it to say. The difficulty is not in finding the appropriate language. The real difficulty is to discover precisely what it is that this supposed collective will wishes enacted.

For, in truth, this supposed 'authority' or 'collective will' is largely an abstraction. It is, as are so many other expressions which we in our daily dialogue conjure up in order to promote the free flow of imprecise discussion (and no democracy can possibly flourish without plenty of this), just one more tag that we employ to describe an impalpable *tertium quid* in order to facilitate thought and controversy on our social and political institutions – very useful controversy, perhaps largely because it is in terms which lack precision, so that everybody, those informed and interested, and those less informed and less interested, can join in, instead of being confined to the select few academic and high-powered thinkers. We really mean by it all those common features that can be isolated and extracted from the whole sum of the individual opinions of citizens in the community; of those who trouble to give expression to their views on public platforms, in the press, in Parliament, on television, and of all those who by their vote in the ballot box, as occasion arises, indicate their agreement or disagreement.

But this collective will is, though largely, not wholly an abstraction; there are some broad objectives which are accepted as desirable by society as a whole. Such objectives are, however, formulated only in general terms, far too general to be embodied in the precise language of a legal concept. It is when society condescends to the particular that the inevitable discord breaks out. 'Thou shalt not covet thy neighbour's . . . ox nor his ass . . . nor anything that is thy neighbour's.' These famous words seem to contain the clearest of imperatives. In other words, respect other people's property and rights and do not greedily appropriate to yourself that to which you have no rightful or moral claim. But in the pattern of a complex modern system of ownership of many types of property of an almost limitless variety, fitted into a welfare state, itself based on a mixed economy with its public and private sectors, nourished and invigorated by acute controversy and conflict over economic 'isms' and cross-interests as to who should have what and how much and why, the application of the general principle to detailed social arrangements leads to the most opposite conclusions according to the standpoint of each individual. It is when the broad principle is applied to the myriad different aspects of practical life that the lawyer, as he addresses himself to the task of draughtsmanship, often asks himself, 'Does "authority" ever exercise a single, consistent will, capable of clear interpretation, in its application to any given actual circumstances?' To this question the answer must be 'comparatively rarely'.

There is hardly such a thing as a coherent, consistent, collective will of the community – rather there is a healthy, intense, often loud-mouthed, even violent dissonance of a multiplicity of different wills. *Quot homines, tot sententiae.* And the social and political mechanism of the press, the public platform, the ballot box and Parliament produces in the end a decision as to what in fact is to be done in any given set of circumstances in face of this discord of wills. It is this decision which the lawyers frame, with more or less difficulty, according as the decision is more or less precise, in legal language.

To the question, therefore, can the law give expression to this collective will of the community in so far as it exists, I answer, yes. Of course, I do not mean that the legal language employed is always free from ambiguity (far less, easy for the non-lawyer to understand). But the courts are there to resolve and adjudicate on problems thrown up by legal ambiguities as and when they come to light, generally when the law in question is applied to circumstances in a given case which were not envisaged when the language was chosen. And it may be that the interpretation put on the ambiguity by the courts results in Parliament's evident intention not being achieved by the language chosen by the lawyers; in which case in due course the matter has to be put right by an alteration in the statute by Parliament. But this imperfection, when the very large field of legal enactment which is annually rendered into legal language is borne in mind, is relatively infrequent. When it does arise, it is often really attributable to the fact that Parliament has not clearly thought out what it is that it wishes to enact.

Secondly, once this collective will, so far as it is ascertainable, has been expressed in unambiguous words in a statute, is that the end of the problem? No, in a sense it is the beginning; because the big problem arises then, can the law, so framed, be enforced? This question is in general part of a larger question – will this law, if enacted, be accepted by the broad mass of the community as sensible on the whole, even if disliked in parts, and on the whole not too oppressive and irksome? This question – could a law in that form be enforced if enacted? – should of course be considered by Parliament and the Executive before it is put on the statute book. Law Officers of the Crown must have warned ministers times out of number that a bill they intended to introduce before Parliament would be incapable of adequate enforcement if passed, because in the long run too many ordinary, reasonable men and women wouldn't stand for it. Generally, ministers defer to that advice.

To take an example that springs to mind, there is always a risk that laws designed to enforce rationing or price control, if too stringent in terms, will only lead to a large black market in the goods in question, 'under the counter'. I am not, of course, arguing that a government should never, particularly in times of crisis, introduce legislation designed to enforce rationing or price control; merely that great care should be taken to avoid making its terms so severe that reasonable people think them oppressive. Sometimes governments have, even in peacetime, to maintain or even introduce rationing control, as did the

1945 Labour Government, for example, in the case of 'red' petrol. This superseded petrol rationing which had been found to be largely inoperable and in consequence was withdrawn. It is greatly against the public interest that such legislation should be enacted unless it is so framed that reasonable people will be ready to obey it. If such enactments do not achieve their objective their habitual disregard tends to bring the law as a whole into disrepute; they act as a kind of constant prod towards dishonesty; they penalise the honest citizen who tries to observe them and advantage the less honest who are ready to circumvent them.

To be enforceable to a sufficient degree – no law is a hundred per cent enforceable – a law must be supported by the approval in principle of the preponderating mass of sensible-minded people. There will always be the less scrupulous who, if their private interests so require, will not hesitate by dishonesty to break the law. The danger point comes if a large number of otherwise honest and respectable citizens think the law so unreasonable that it does not strain their consciences to break it. A law which will not command such support should not be put on the statute book. Respect for the rule of law is one of the greatest contributions the British genius has made to civilised living and the instinct in Britons is very deeply rooted to obey the law. But the law in this context means to them a law which, besides being enacted by Parliament, has common sense behind it and is not oppressive. We should strive hard to preserve British respect for the rule of law and avoid passing laws which put a strain on that feeling of respect. Is this all no more than a solid but pedestrian truism? Is it not obvious, without discussion, that there are some things the law can do and some that it cannot? I would answer, yes; but it is not so obvious what type of things can and cannot be done by enacting laws. To take one possible example, at the outset, one may turn to United States history.

Students of American history can judge whether it was the collective will of the United States community that the United States should go 'dry' or whether prohibition was forced upon an unwilling public opinion by an Administration and Congress out of touch with it. If it were the latter there can be few more striking examples of what happens when 'authority', in the sense I am using the word, seeks to attain its purpose by passing laws which large numbers of honest and respectable persons think do not make sense. When sensible persons think to themselves, 'I daresay alcohol does cause harm and maybe we would all be healthier and better if we never touched a drink – but I and mine like it and use it in moderation. We resent being pushed about by do-gooders, and we mean to have it whatever the law says', the red light should go up for the lawyer and he should retire from the unequal combat before people defy him in large numbers and lose respect for him. When the prohibition laws were repealed the rot had gone far enough; but history was furnished with a very valuable warning and example of what the law can do and cannot do.

Fiscal legislation perhaps also has a special relevance in this context. By and large, in this country we pay our taxes even if we grumble. We feel contempt for those among us who bilk their fellow citizens by dishonestly not contributing the share of tax apportioned to them by our tax legislation. It may be that, as things stand at the moment, there is some of what I would call perfectly 'lawful resistance', as by a worker who refuses to come in on a Saturday morning merely to earn tax money to pay the Chancellor or the industrialist who refuses to invest and expand because he thinks too much of his profit will go in tax. Opinions differ as to the effect of our present tax system in this context and I do not join in the controversy whether taxes are too high or too low. But there is (and whatever their political allegiances, few would dispute this) an enormous potential field for increased public expenditure to the extent that our economy can afford it. Although our country has a record to be proud of we are far from being the ideal state, whether education, housing, health or social benefits are concerned. The State, by common acceptance, claims through taxes its share of our income in order to finance this highly desirable expenditure.

The heavier the tax the more we complain, until we get used to the tax. Most of us take such steps as the law allows us to avoid or lessen the incidence of the tax burden upon us; but it is only a smallish minority among us who are prepared dishonestly and contrary to law to evade it. But woe betide the day, or days if they should ever come, when taxes multiply so that respect for them declines; when respectable citizens begin to sympathise with those caught out trying to evade them dishonestly; when the reasonable, ordinary man, 'the man on the Clapham omnibus', as he has sometimes been called, begins to think that only a mug pays all the taxes which Parliament enacts that he should pay. Happily, if that is an acceptable term in relation to the subject of taxes, whilst we differ violently as to what is the proper level of taxes and their proper form we (except for a small number of disreputables) agree that whatever the fiscal law requires us to pay we must pay, much as it may hurt, and console ourselves with a good grumble. Our national habit of vigorous and uninhibited discussion of our taxes in Parliament and press I think constitutes a major safeguard in this country (I do not speak of other countries) which preserves our national mood of paying honestly though grumbling hard; and it is not, I believe, being starry-eyed to think, as I do, that dishonest evasion takes place within narrow limits. But if ever personal dishonesty in tax matters became the rule, not the exception, it would I am sure betoken a serious breakdown of our civic morality and our fiscal law and beget a poison that would spread through and corrupt our way of life. Our Chancellors of all persuasions have fortunately shown themselves fully aware of the dangers of extending the fiscal law beyond the point when reasonable people feel morally bound to obey it.

There is some talk these days about the possibility of introducing a 'wealth tax'. As it has been described, it would be an annual tax of one per cent or more on the aggregate capital value of the taxpayer's assets in excess of a specified amount – £20,000 has been mentioned. Sometimes it is said that there should be some exclusions from the taxpayer's assets which would have to be evaluated for this purpose, such as the capital value of his home, if he owns a house. Whether assets such as goodwill, copyright, trade secrets, stock, the capital value of pension rights or similar assets would be excluded I do not know. It is not within my terms of reference to discuss what economic consequences such a tax might have; but I believe that, if authority will it, our law could not operate it, or at best could operate it only most ineffectively. I know it exists in other countries. How it operates in those countries I do not know – accounts differ. But if introduced in this country, in the form above indicated, I think it would constitute a constant and potent stimulus to defiance of the law and downright dishonesty in evading its provisions. To expect taxpayers, year in and year out, to put a value on such things as pictures hanging on their walls, furniture, copyright in books, rights under an agreement to receive royalties in respect of the use of a patent, and all the other miscellaneous assets people possess, the values of which vary from year to year, and are largely a matter of opinion, depending on 'what you can get for them', is, to my mind, to issue them a standing and pressing invitation, in their own interest, to be not too scrupulous and little by little to slip into habits of semi-dishonest, then dishonest, undervaluation.

An evaluation of assets once in a generation on death for assessment of death duties presents enough difficulties. But an annual evaluation has frightening possibilities. My own view is that those who believe further steps are necessary for ironing out inequalities in wealth (I express no view as to whether or not such steps should be undertaken) will be imposing a great strain on the law if they depart from the yardstick of income to the measurement by which the law is well-accustomed and have resort to capital values as the yardstick for the purposes of annual assessments. How, for example, if at all, would cash standing to the credit of an active current account, upon which drawings are made daily or from week to week, or overdrafts, be taken into account in evaluating the taxpayer's total assets? On their amount at the beginning or end of the tax year? Or on a yearly average? Or possibly not at all? It is sometimes said by supporters of the wealth tax that it is necessary because estate duty has no – or an inadequate – result for the purpose of ironing out gross inequalities of wealth, since estate duty is no more than a 'voluntary tax' because it is so easy to evade. To the extent that it can be evaded, this could, I believe, be wholly or substantially stopped by the appropriate changes in the tax code. But if estate duty, in the form described, is a 'voluntary tax', surely a wealth tax, in the form described above, would be infinitely more so.

If the tax is to take the form indicated above, the law, I believe, let alone the tax administration, will not be able to cope. Over the years, if the tax stayed, it would lead, I believe, to a steady decline in public morality as bad as any 'expenses racket', and wide-scale evasion and unenforceability. This sort of thing, I think, constitutes a dangerous and insidious type of defiance of the law. Authority, as a tax gatherer, would have to be told firmly by lawyers that 'this is a matter in which you cannot give effect to your will by process of law'.

The feeling which underlies the citizens' resentment at the Chancellor's annual claims upon him is basically one of vexation at being told what he is to do with what he regards as his own money. He dislikes interference in a sphere which he considers as the proper sphere of his own choice; though he reluctantly accepts that such interference is, in his own and the national interest, unavoidable. It is not that taxes, high though they may be, leave him impoverished. If he is in employment, after paying his taxes he still, except in the case of some of the lower paid, enjoys living standards and can permit himself a scale of personal expenditure which is the envy of most of the rest of the world. He would probably resent having to pay income tax even if the standard rate of income tax were again one shilling in the pound. For, however desirable the social purpose which the Government seeks to accomplish, the liege, with his stubborn sense of independence, questions the right of the lawmaker to regulate beyond a certain point what he regards as the proper sphere of his own choice in his own conduct.

To some extent this is the case with laws which entrench on the field of personal private behaviour in which the citizen feels he should be guided by his own sense of moral restraint and private conscience. We recently enacted that homosexual behaviour between consenting male adults should, except in a limited range, no longer constitute a criminal offence. Basically, why did we do so? No parents would contemplate with equanimity the prospect of their sons growing up into homosexuals. Apart from those who are temperamentally homosexual, very few ordinary men and women, such as one expects to meet 'on the top of the Clapham omnibus', would view homosexual behaviour as other than behaviour which, to say the least of it, should be very strongly discouraged. 'Authority' was and is very definitely against homosexual behaviour.

If so, why does not authority, with the aid of Parliament, continue to say through the criminal law, 'such behaviour is not to be'? It is not as if such behaviour was viewed by authority as being of no general importance so far as the broad public interest was concerned. On the contrary, it was denounced as corrupting, decadent and of exceedingly evil influence and likely to spread its influence unless checked by a continuing criminal sanction. The controversy whether it should cease, as between consenting male adults, to be a criminal offence was for years fast and furious. Authority could huff and bluff and blow out its cheeks, deploring homosexual behaviour and denouncing those who proposed a change in the law. Many thought it quite sufficient, in order to demolish the case for change, to embark upon a constant and sonorous repetition of the word 'sodomy' with a hiss. On the other side it was argued that, if the law were changed, it would put an end to the blackmail to which homosexuals are subject. Personally I do not believe it will – certainly not entirely; to be a homosexual will, I think, still be, in the opinion of the vast majority of people, a matter for opprobrium, or at least of great misfortune, which those who engage in homosexual practices would be ready to pay to keep secret. And it was argued that the law which makes such conduct an offence can be flouted with impunity. But equally the law says theft is a crime, but there will always be thieves; yet no one would seriously argue that for this reason, the Larceny Act, 1916, should be repealed. The law can discourage homosexualism and punish those who, practising it, are caught out; just as it discourages a great percentage of potential thieves.

I am far from saying that these and like arguments have no substance; on the contrary I think they have very great substance. But I do not myself think that basically it was for these reasons that (with some exceptions) it was made no longer an offence as between consenting adults. Seduction, the perverting of the young by those older, of course, is still an offence. The change, I think, was made because the liege felt that this was not fit stuff for the criminal law. It was one of those matters of private judgment and conduct in which each must be guided by his own conscience and decision, taken voluntarily without compulsion – a topic with which the criminal law should not meddle, as being none of its business, but stand away at a respectful distance. He regards himself as endowed with a will and purpose of his own by which in a wide range of relationships he will regulate his own behaviour. Advice from his friends and parents he will welcome or, at least, tolerate but not advice from lawyers, much less compulsion. And, as this was gradually borne in on authority, so was it recognised that here again was another boundary in human affairs beyond which the criminal law should not stray and would not in the long run be either tolerated or respected if it did. In consequence it prudently withdrew.

Not wholly dissimilar, I think, is the attitude of the great majority of people on the law in its application to adultery. Adulterous behaviour is possibly in the case of a lamentable few almost a habit; in the view of some it is not much worse than a peccadillo; but in the eyes of the vast majority of people it is, unless there are mitigating circumstances, conduct which is seriously reprehensible. To break up another man's home by adulterous behaviour is to do him a grievous wrong. Beyond doubt, 'authority' is very definitely against adultery. No doubt, the law annexes certain consequences to it by way of relief to the spouse who has been wronged, such as dissolution of marriage and damages. But the general condemnation of adultery goes far beyond its aspect as a wrong to individuals. It is wrong to the community as a whole. Authority regards and rightly regards the institution of marriage and family life as fundamental to a happy and stable community. Then why, again, does not authority in this country, as is done in some other countries, seek through Parliament to discourage it by making adulterous behaviour a criminal offence? Why is not authority tidy and logical?

I feel sure that any such proposal in this country would attract little, if any, support. Most people would think it had something almost trogloditish about it. But why would people reject it? I do not share the view of cynics that it is because they or their friends have indulged or might in the future be tempted to indulge in such behaviour, even if some might be influenced by this kind of consideration. It is not a case of 'There but for the grace of God go I'. I think the real reason, again, would be a deeper feeling that here, also, was something which however morally wrong was not the concern of the criminal law but the proper subject of private and personal restraint without legal compulsion. 'That is not what the criminal law is for,' most would think to themselves; though they would probably find it difficult to put into words their precise reason for so thinking. They would find it difficult, because they would be actuated by a perhaps somewhat irrational but deep-rooted instinct as to what was and what was not appropriate matter for the criminal law in the kind of society in which they wished to live.

One can imagine a dialogue between a questioner and an ordinary, typical, right-minded citizen: *Questioner:* 'Do you agree that it is disgraceful behaviour to commit adultery?' *Citizen:* 'Yes, most certainly, except possibly in cases where there are mitigating circumstances.' *Questioner:* 'Behaviour which is not only disgraceful but which may cause great harm and misery?' *Citizen:* 'Yes, generally.' *Questioner:* 'Should not respectable people be protected from such behaviour?' *Citizen:* 'Yes, if possible.' *Questioner:* 'Should not therefore the act of adultery be made a criminal offence? Is not this the best way to deter adulterers?' The overwhelming answer would, I think, be that, whether or not it would be the best way of deterring adulterers, it would be absurd to make adultery a crime. If the answer is given that the wronged spouse is amply compensated by the law giving him or her a right to have his or her marriage dissolved and even to recover damages, this does not answer the question, 'Why not go further, and by making adultery a crime, make it less likely that the act of adultery will be committed? Why shut the stable door only after the horse has gone?' The real answer is that if good sense and good feeling won't stop it, nevertheless the criminal law has nothing – and should have nothing – to do with this area of behaviour. It is the area in which the individual must, as an exercise of his own will and his own choice, restrain himself from behaviour which hurts others. This, therefore, again is an instance of authority willing strongly that such behaviour should not take place but realising that the law, at least the criminal law, is not an apt instrument for enforcing its will.

Perhaps not wholly different considerations influence people's thinking about the law of obscenity, as manifested in the periodic controversies that arise in the press and elsewhere, when a publication of note comes before the courts to be adjudged obscene or otherwise. A robust refusal on the part of numberless stubborn-minded individuals to be told by authority what they may and what they may not read has happily over recent years kept the law within reasonable limits and prevented what might otherwise have developed into a melancholy and humourless procession of literary works of merit to the execution block of puritan unreason.

I hope I shall not be thought to be taking a too far-fetched example if I refer to the practice of smoking cigarettes. However we view authority, however inarticulate the collective will of the community, it is against cancer as firmly as President Coolidge's clergyman was against sin. Doctors continually press upon us that cigarette smoking causes, or at least strongly predisposes to, the contracting of throat and lung cancer. Why, then, should not the law-giver say to himself, 'Well, then, let the law stop smoking – let those who smoke be punished'? Some may disagree; but, I think, the vast majority of reasonable people would think that simply to state the proposition, 'cigarette smoking is a crime', is to demonstrate its absurdity. Sensible, law-abiding citizens would flatly refuse to obey a law which made cigarette smoking a crime. If asked why they refused, few would even bother to give a reasoned answer to the effect that such a law constituted an unreasonable intrusion upon what should be an area of private choice for the individual – their answer would be shorter and simpler, namely, 'whatever the law says I mean to smoke if I choose and the law can go hang'. Even if the law-giver tried some more subtle legal pressure to stop smoking – for example, if he were Chancellor of the Exchequer and in his Budget raised taxes on tobacco so high that cigarette smoking became impossible for ordinary, private budgets, there would, I am sure, be an outcry. He would be told, 'Mr. Chancellor, stick to your text – you, as Chancellor, may use your Budget to raise revenue, and influence the pattern of our economy, but not to constitute yourself a *censor morum*'.

A striking example of this unsuitability or inadequacy of the law is to be found, I think, in the field of international law, as laid down in the Charter of the United Nations. 'Authority', if this is not too elusive a concept in the field of international relations, willed certain things. It was the ardent longing of countless millions of human beings the world over that the horrors of war should cease for ever and that differences between nations should be resolved by peaceful means. It seemed such elementary common sense; and surely it is legitimate to regard, in the international sphere, the firm determination of all people of goodwill on the earth's surface that an end should be made of war, and that the means of bringing this about should be found by creating the United Nations Organisation based on the Charter, as constituting or bringing into being a kind of international 'authority' of united wills. It is no more of an abstraction than that collective will which is supposed to constitute 'authority' in the case of a single national community.

Yet, even at the outset, when the representatives of the nations got down to the work of framing the Charter in San Francisco in 1945, they tacitly accepted that however self-obviously desirable were the broad objectives of the Charter there was a point beyond which international processes of law, as formulated in the Charter, could not go to achieve them. They accepted this limitation when they incorporated in the Charter the principle of the 'veto'. The General Assembly was to be the debating chamber of the world, empowered to make recommendations which would carry a mighty weight of moral force behind them. But it was in the Security Council alone that power was vested to decide and embark on executive action to enforce the will of the United Nations Organisation in its struggle to achieve the noble objectives which were its *raison d'être*. Yet there was to be power to 'veto' the decisions of the

Security Council on all matters of major importance (everything except procedural matters). Such decisions could be taken only by a majority of seven including the unanimous vote of the five major permanent members of the Security Council; and if any one of the five declined to agree, the Security Council was powerless to proceed to a major decision. Those who framed the Charter inserted the veto provision because they felt bound to recognise that a nation, if its vital interests ran contrary to what perhaps the whole world wished and all other members of the Security Council were ready to decree, just would not conform. So it had to be given the power by its veto to frustrate the will of international 'authority'.

We all know how the power has been used, and not only by Soviet Russia, but by Great Britain herself at the time of Suez. It was not a power given only to nations who in the international sphere could be regarded as the counterpart of the rapscallions or misfits in domestic society who for one reason or another will not conform to the will of society, because they always 'know better' than the vast majority of their fellow citizens, or think they do, or are criminally inclined, but to the august five nations themselves whose representatives permanently sit as members of the Security Council. What is this other than enabling these nations to say, 'We support the United Nations objectives and will most certainly obey the framework of international law as laid down by the Charter, upon obedience to which law the achievement of those objectives depends, provided always, of course, that we freely and voluntarily agree to obey that law – and we may not always agree.' What a humiliating, but nevertheless what an unavoidable, acceptance of the melancholy truth that, however firm and clear the will of authority, however solidly based on common sense and good feeling, there is nevertheless a sharp and equally clear limitation to the power of law to enforce that will.

Moreover, to take another example on a rather different plane, but still in the international sphere, the International Court which sits at the Hague is itself an organ of the United Nations. How ardently we all hoped that this was to be the supreme world tribunal before which, by due process of a continually evolving code of international law, disputes

H

between nations were to be resolved peaceably according to law. The Court's mandate was, in case of need, to be enforced by action through the Security Council, functioning as a kind of international bailiff (provided, of course, it was not hindered by an exercise of the veto). No word of mine is intended in any sense as a criticism of the very excellent judges who man and have manned that Court, and the courage and independence they have consistently shown in their great work to sustain and augment the role of international law as the supreme determinant of international disputes. But as early as 1948 history was plainly warning against expecting too much of this or any other court. Moussadeq and his colleagues, contrary to law, or at least without making it plain that they were going to comply with what international law required as a condition of their action, namely prompt payment of compensation, undertook to nationalise the Abadan refinery. The British Government referred the matter to the International Court. That Court, at Britain's request, after argument before the Court, exercised its jurisdiction by making a declaration that, until the whole question could be brought before the Court for final determination on the merits, neither party, Britain or Persia, should take any further step likely to prejudice the interim position. Here, to everybody's satisfaction, at any rate in this country, was international law asserting itself in a major international dispute. This was what the rule of law meant – here was a real pointer to the future. Sharp disillusion set in when the Persian Government promptly announced that it proposed to take no notice of the Court's recommendation; and it was painfully but pellucidly obvious that nothing at all could be done about this announcement.

Voices were even raised in criticism of the British Government's decision to refer the dispute to the Court when all that could emerge from a successful reference was an unenforceable recommendation, hardly worth the paper it was written on. History was plainly saying, 'Do not raise your hopes too high; excellent as is the Court, splendid as is the international purpose which led to its establishment, and unanswerable as is the case of international authority in support of the arbitrament of international differences by rule of law, the unpalatable truth

is that, if you put too heavy a burden on the Court, all you will
do is to break its back. The law can only go so far. Do not, by
entrusting the Court with the determination of disputes on
which feelings run too high, bring into bleak contrast the high
mission of the Court with its comparative impotence to enforce
its decree.'

The case which came before the Court in 1946 relating to
the mining of British warships in the Corfu Channel has also,
I think, a somewhat melancholy relevance in this context. Two
British warships, peacefully steaming through the Corfu
Channel, were mined and seriously damaged. There was heavy
loss of life among the crews. Great Britain had reason to believe
that the Government of Albania was responsible for this out-
rage. No doubt in Palmerston's day gunboats would have been
sent to the coast of Albania; instead, in 1946, the Law Officers
of the Crown were sent to the Hague to establish the guilt of
Albania before the International Court and to claim compensation on behalf of Britain. There was a lengthy hearing with
a great deal of evidence called. The question whether responsibility could be lawfully proved to attach to Albania was duly
investigated by all proper judicial processes before the Court.
Finally, after a full hearing, the Court came to the conclusion
that Albania's responsibility was proved and awarded a substantial sum to Great Britain by way of compensation. From that
day to this it has been quite impossible for the British Government to secure payment of this sum. The judgment remains
still unsatisfied, equivalent really to no more than a strong moral
condemnation of Albania.

Here again it has been found impossible to enforce the law
and the Government of Albania has from that day to this stood
completely at defiance. It is, perhaps, not an overstatement to
say that the Abadan Refinery case and the Corfu Channel case
were the two cases of possible major international implications
in which Great Britain has been involved seeking to establish
that a wrong has been done to her and to seek redress from the
Court. It is true that in the Abadan case the Court, when the
matter came before it on the substantive merit of the case,
ultimately decided that it had no jurisdiction; but this does not
in any sense derogate from the fact that its preliminary recom-

mendation of a *status quo* was wholly ignored by the Government of Persia. In these two major cases, therefore, in which Britain was engaged and in which it was essential that the rule of international law should be affirmed and upheld, there was open, unashamed and wholly unjustifiable refusal on the part of those against whom the Court pronounced to comply with the judgment of the Court. As one of the Law Officers concerned in these two cases, I hope I may be excused if I dilate unduly on the sharp and vivid sense of disappointment felt at the time, particularly at the Persian Government's defiance of the Court's recommendation in the Abadan Refinery case, by many people of all shades of opinion – I remember so well the sudden and bleak realisation that international law could do so much less for us than we all hoped. Here was a major failure on the part of international law and it seems to me directly relevant to the theme which I am pursuing that law can function as an effective instrument for the achievement of the will of authority only within certain closely drawn limits. It must be the endeavour of mankind to extend these limits as the years go by and so make the law truly effective.

Since these two cases, I believe, governments have become more conscious of the risk, lest if issues so grave are regularly referred to the Court, and if the moral authority that goes with its decisions is not sufficient to secure compliance by the nation against whom the decision goes, the result may well be that the Court will decline in influence and respect and come to be looked on as a suitable tribunal for the decision only of minor international boundary disputes and questions that do not really matter a great deal to the nations in dispute. Happily that situation is still remote – let us hope that it will never eventuate. But we should be vigilant to avoid placing the Court in a situation which leads to a loss of confidence in it; and one precaution that I think we should observe for this purpose is not to expect too much from the Court in its early and formative years – and in terms of history these are still very early years in the life of the International Court. In other words, here again is a context most critical to the future peace and happiness of the world in which we must recognise that the law is, and for the foreseeable future will remain, an imperfect instrument for the achievement of many of the most urgent purposes of 'authority', conceived as the combined will of human beings united in a deep yearning and determination to substitute reason for violence, the courts for the battlefield, in the future clashes of interest of the peoples of the world without which history would not exist.

At the present time, hard-pressed ministers are grappling bravely on our behalf with the most daunting problems of many kinds, to two of which I would like now to make reference as having, I think, some relevance to my theme. It would be a poor service if I said anything which might possibly have the effect of making their task in the slightest degree more difficult, should any reader persevere as far as these lines; and nothing is further from my intention. I do no more than pose questions which perhaps raise matters worth reflecting upon. The two types of problems to which I refer are some relating to the economic measures upon which the Government is currently engaged and some arising from the question of race relations, centring upon immigration from the Commonwealth. First, an aspect of the economic measures.

The pound has from time to time come under strain – we have had devaluation. Overseas holders of sterling have tended to think we spend too much on ourselves and don't produce enough to earn our standard of living. It would be the collective will of society that we should make certain of deriving the maximum benefit from our price advantage in foreign markets resulting from devaluation, notably by cutting our national cloth according to what we can allow ourselves to spend of our national income, consistently with freeing resources and effort in sufficient measure to support an export-led boom. How far is the law a serviceable instrument to achieve this objective? How far must broad-based consent and spontaneous endeavour be looked to as a means of bringing this about? Men and women whom we loosely regard and describe as 'organised labour', if you add the members of their families, amount in numbers to something not very far short of half the community. The scale of their incomes is an important element in the cost of our products to overseas buyers and the freeing of resources for exports. Since 1964 the Government has made

Herculean efforts to inaugurate an incomes policy relating incomes to what our scale of production enables us to afford – a policy based almost wholly on mutual agreement and consent between both sides of industry, with government help. It went further in the difficult months of 1966 when the Government and Parliament activated in October 1966 Part IV of the Prices and Incomes Act 1966 for the remainder of one year only, with its provisions which might have resulted in wage earners, who would not conform to the desired wage pattern, being subjected to a criminal sanction. The year has long since expired, but the problem of matching our incomes to our production is still with us in an acute form – in a perhaps less acute form it may be with us for some years; so long as we try to maintain high and rising living standards, ample social services and a world role (even if substantially reduced) in defence and in other directions.

Understandably the Government are desperately and rightly anxious to achieve moderation in wage increases on a basis of consent without a legal, still more a criminal, sanction. It is not so very difficult by consent or, if unavoidable, by legal compulsion to control or limit dividend increases, still less so rents, and in general, by fiscal measures, salaries can be kept within limits. But if, when all this is done, when every possible effort has been made by the T.U.C., the Government, and by leaders of individual, nation-wide unions to achieve restraint in wage growth by broad-based consent, nevertheless the nation's effort is held up and even frustrated by unreasonable or wild-cat strike action in support of demands for wage increases, would it be feasible for the law to say that fines and imprisonment should be the result?

Here I would draw a distinction between the short term and the long term. In a highly critical short-term period it may be the Government can, in this country at any rate, impose its will for a limited time by legislation which in the long term would be rejected as intolerably harsh and draconian. Part IV of the Prices and Incomes Act 1966, to which I have referred, was perhaps an example of this. Also, I do not say that possibly by other more gentle legal expedients of a civil character as distinct from a criminal character an influence on wage growth might not be exercised. For example, I have seen it suggested that the immunities which the existing law at present accords should in future be accorded only to trade unions which are registered and presumably comply with prescribed tests required for registering. So to enact would probably involve placing in the hands of the public officer, whoever he may be, charged with the responsibility of deciding what unions qualified for registration, power so formidable as to be unacceptable to public opinion; unless indeed such powers were so hedged around with limitations as to make them virtually ineffective.

As I write, the recommendations of the Donovan Royal Commission on Trade Unions are not yet available and I write in ignorance of what may be the proposals contained in the report being prepared by Lord Donovan and his colleagues. Of course the report may suggest solutions which render most of what is written here otiose. But, in general, I think it is not too difficult to frame and put into legal form systems which in the field of wage and salary increases provide for 'early warning' or 'cooling off' periods. But the ultimate question will always still remain, 'How are laws which embody such systems to be enforced? What is to be the sanction to compel compliance in the event of disobedience on a small or large scale or even wholesale defiance? Is it to be a possible liability to be imprisoned or fined?' This, for the purpose of my theme, is really the acid test. 'Aye, there's the rub.' Can authority through the law say to the wage or salary earner (as part of the long-term structure of our legislation), 'If you don't conform to the income scheme, you may be fined or sent to prison'? I do not say that in the history of a nation situations – even long-term situations – might not arise in which a government has to say to itself, 'Needs must – we will have to chance introducing this legislation; we must say to would-be defiers, "We shall have to see who is stronger, you or the law backed by authority. Do your worst and see what happens." ' Indeed, it is possibly arguable that the present is not so far from being one of those times. The Government, fearful of the appalling prospects that may face the nation if devaluation fails, have announced that in order to ensure that their prices and incomes policy works they would introduce legislation if necessary and so far as necessary to control, *inter alia*, the rise in wage incomes, in order to make certain it does not exceed the nation's economic capacity.*

I do not here enter into the controversy whether or not such control should, in spite of all, rest on a voluntary instead of a compulsive basis. But if the Government are right, that in the ultimate resort compulsive legal powers must be available to them, is the present a situation in which they are called upon by the gravity of the country's predicament to say to the lawyer, 'Draft the necessary texts', and to Parliament, through its majority, 'Put them on the statute book'? Government must, it can be argued, in some periods of national crisis, within reason of course, have its way by means of the law, and cherished private freedoms must yield in the face of the truism that there is no such formidable enemy of public and private freedom as anarchy and chaos springing from weak government. In such times those must bear a heavy moral responsibility who refuse to recognise that there are circumstances when the exigencies of government in a democracy require that those in power cause the enactment of laws which in other times would be regarded as altogether too great an encroachment on the sphere of individual liberty and make full use of the powers such laws confer upon them.

Before the war I remember being shocked at press headlines, saying, in effect, 'Mussolini succeeded in doing so, Hitler succeeded in doing so – why can't we?' The reference was not to the crimes and brutalities those ruffians perpetrated, but to measures they took, arguably, from some points of view, in the public interest of the peoples over whom they were dictators; and the implication was that by contrast with them democracy was no better than a 'talking shop', incapable of drastic action to safeguard the nation in an emergency. Such talk can be dangerous – it was dangerous in the thirties, when the thinking and moods it expressed could have become the Achilles' heel of democracy. Happily this Achilles' heel is now solidly buttressed round, at any rate in the free countries, by a protective covering of common sense and mature political judgment born of bitter experience of authoritarian rule by millions of human beings tragically affected by it in the course of the twentieth

* This was written before the text of the Prices and Incomes Act 1968 became available.

century. Happily, also, we are far from the 'thirties, and the free countries, at any rate, are very far from that type of thinking.

What is the other side? If any Government, as part of the permanent pattern of our legislation, decided to introduce sanctions which could result in the infliction of severe penalties upon union leaders and rank and file who proffered and sought to enforce wage claims, even if without any merit or popular sympathy or in breach of negotiated agreements, what, one may anticipate, would be the chances of survival of such legislation in the long term? Suppose that legislation of that kind, not limited in time, but permanent in form, were enacted and, though reluctantly assented to by Parliament and public opinion, perhaps during a crisis, it remained on the statute book, and was in force in calmer times thereafter. How might it fare? For some time, possibly, its existence would be forgotten, no occasion arising to seek to put it into effect. Then an industrial dispute occurs which gives rise to strike action contrary to the provisions of the Act.

What is at issue is a valued fundamental right, deeply and increasingly prized, ever since the repeal in the last century of the laws with regard to conspiracy as they then applied to combination for trade union purposes, namely, the right to withhold one's labour and combine in order jointly to protect and improve the living standards of oneself, one's family and those engaged in rendering a like service by their work to the community. Put otherwise, perhaps in an over-simplified form, the issue is: can authority ever make one man work for another by threatening him with fines and imprisonment if he refuses, whether alone or in combination with others, to do so? So to state the issue is to make it obvious at once that any proposal to impinge on this fundamental right must be approached with extreme caution and, in general, undertaken only in exceptional circumstances. It must be remembered, too, that what may look to authority irrational and extravagant strike action may look to those concerned the very opposite, a hundred per cent justified and, indeed, imperative. There may have been – I don't for a moment suggest there always are – pin-pricks which over a period of time may have goaded those concerned to

growing, though unexpressed, resentment; it may be culmin-
ating perhaps in some overwhelming act by an insensitive
management which seemed to the workers concerned to be
altogether intolerable; pin-pricks unknown to the public at
large and not easy for the workers concerned or their leaders to
explain and 'put over' to the outside world so as to be generally
understood.

That is one side of it. The other side is that, in the circumstances of the supposed dispute, strike action might be likely to
do serious harm to the national economy, and ministers must
after all cope – 'Government must govern'. Though ministers
are there to be belaboured by public criticism – none of them
would complain of that – critics in a more kindly mood might
ponder on the truth of one very admirable and distinguished
Minister of Labour's *cri de cœur*, that his task was 'like a bed
of nails'. They will all know how quickly and fundamentally
public sympathy can change round.

The organisers of strike action in the assumed circumstances
may have been cast by authority in the role of arch ogres for
having organised 'wildcat' strike action deeply inimical to the
public interest. A prosecution takes place, probably on the
direction of a rather hesitant Attorney-General. There may be
expected to be plenty of press publicity and photographs of
those concerned. When those charged appear in court they
don't look like ogres at all, but are obviously plain, ordinary
men, sincerely fighting for what they consider is due to their
members to whom they owe a responsibility. One prosecution
takes place; then, perhaps after an interval, another. Legislation which, when tempers were high, may have seemed
necessary, begins to look intolerably harsh. A groundswell of
public resentment gets under way. As the well-liked local trade
unionist leaves his home to go to the Court, sympathy streams
towards him from the neighbours. Admiring well-wishers walk
back with him to his home after the local magistrates have
imposed an 'intolerably harsh' fine which anyhow is paid by a
whip-round of his friends. The point may even be reached
when demonstrations on his behalf take place which authority
may think as unreasonable as those mounted for the Tichborne
claimant in the last century, but do not appear to be so to

large sections of opinion moved by the simple human logic:
'Never mind what the law says; he may have broken it, but he
is a decent, honest man, victimised for doing what he thinks to
be right – it is outrageous to punish him for it.' Many, perhaps
many thousands, of persons who were involved in the dispute
may have been just as responsible as he is. But in the nature of
things it is only feasible to pick out a few, perhaps three or four,
local union representatives for prosecution and it will seem
intolerably unfair to single out a few from very many 'to carry
the can' for the others. I simply pose these difficulties with the
observation that such legislation is apt to recoil on those who
enact it and try to enforce it.

Something of the sort happened in the case of Order 1305, a
war-time order designed to curb strike action so as not to
inhibit the nation's war-time effort. The 1945 Labour Government inherited it on coming into office as part of the war-time
legislation and subordinate legislation still in force when the
war came to an end.

Order 1305 made it a criminal offence to provoke or bring
about strike action unless certain procedures were first complied
with which might have the effect of heading the strike off
through conciliation by the Ministry of Labour and eventual
arbitration. The Order had legislative effect and was part of
the law of the land. Experience shows that such legislation puts
the Attorney-General in a very difficult position. Infringements
of the law occur which constitute criminal offences. At question
time in the House of Commons the Attorney-General is asked
whether the infringement has been reported to him and
whether he proposes to require the Director of Public Prosecutions to institute criminal proceedings. No Attorney-General,
responsible as he is for the due overall enforcement of the
criminal law through the supervisory control which he exercises
over the Director of Public Prosecutions, could adopt a public
stance of disregarding habitual breaches of the criminal law.
By virtue of his office he would in due course be obliged to
direct that prosecutions should be instituted where cases were
concerned in which a breach of the criminal law could be
proved. No doubt, in the circumstances of a particular case he
may, if he thinks there are adequate reasons of public (as

distinct from party political) interest for so doing, refrain in the exercise of his discretion from causing criminal proceedings to be instituted. But, if legislation of the type in question were in force, and repeated infringements took place, he would before long have to prosecute, however indignant the reaction of the public or a section of the public may be. The result would probably be that he would be held up as a monster of public repression of fundamental human rights and it would be far from certain that he would obtain a conviction from a jury of ordinary men and women who, on the broad human principle that sometimes the law is an ass and goes too far, would refuse to convict. Before very long it would become a case either of the Attorney-General shirking his plain duty or of the relevant legislation being removed from the statute book.

In other countries legislation of this kind exists; but I am speaking of probable reactions of public opinion in this country. Circumstances might develop which would make it inevitable that penal sanctions for strike action should as a permanent (not temporary) feature of our legislation be put on the Statute Book: I just do not know and can only hope not. It may be that non-criminal sanctions could also be devised by lawyers. But I believe public opinion in this country would be very slow indeed to accept the idea that a *bona-fide* trade unionist should ever in normal times be sent to prison because he took part in a strike. It may therefore be that here is another example of a case in which authority has to be told that the criminal law, at any rate, must just keep off the grass and that, though legal draftsmen can draft any number of Order 1305s, this is another sphere of human behaviour for the regulation of which, however much authority may feel tempted to use it, the criminal law is an inept instrument.

As I have said, the second group of problems to which I would refer concerns race relations, centring upon immigration from the Commonwealth. It is not within my terms of reference to discuss the immense moral and social and, indeed, economic issues involved; my task is a narrow one, limited to an examination how far the law in this field can help authority to achieve its purpose. Although there are some who approach these problems on semi-fascist lines it is nevertheless obviously true, I think, that authority, in the sense in which earlier I have sought to define the term, wishes and intends all sections of the community, whether indigenous or immigrant, to live peaceably together in friendly and orderly relationships, all profiting by the service and labour of each without the incessant searing wounds to the spirit that are inflicted by discriminatory conduct and dislike of a man because of something he cannot help. To achieve this situation authority wills that there should be accorded to immigrants from the Commonwealth who have been accepted into the community and have made their homes here opportunities, particularly in employment facilities in the broad sense, and personal respect equal to and neither more nor less than those accorded to the rest of the community. How far can the law serve to bring this about? How far would legislation designed to further these objectives be likely to match up to the test which I earlier ventured to propound, namely that it must be supported in principle by the preponderating mass of sensible-minded people?

The Race Relations Act 1965 provides criminal penalties for deliberate incitement to racial hatred. When this was first proposed it was argued that it involved an unjustifiable invasion of the right of free speech. Public opinion, I believe, does not so regard it and accepts the sections of the Act in which the relevant provisions are embodied as a useful and necessary part of our legislation in the field of the maintenance of public order. But the Act also contains provisions designed to prevent discriminatory practices directed against particular racial, national or ethnic groups in their treatment in places which in a broad sense are provided for access by the general public – all the public. For instance, its purpose was to prevent publicans refusing to serve drinks to customers in public houses on the ground that they were coloured.

As first introduced, the Bill which subsequently became the Race Relations Act, 1965, provided a criminal sanction against this type of discrimination. It was soon made plain after the text of the Bill was available that parliamentary and public opinion, whilst prepared to accept that such practices should be prevented, was not ready to see a criminal sanction as the appropriate method of enforcing these provisions. As a consequence, the Government, in a revised version of the Bill, substituted for the criminal sanctions a procedure by way of reconciliation. There were to be set up conciliation committees which, in the event of complaints about this sort of discrimination, were to endeavour to bring about an amicable settlement between the parties involved. If efforts at conciliation were not successful the matter could be referred to a central Race Relations Board. After examination the Board could, if it thought appropriate, perhaps in a stubborn case that could not be otherwise resolved, report the matter to the Attorney-General. The Attorney-General could ask the courts to pronounce an injunction forbidding those concerned to continue the discriminatory practice in question; and if there were disobedience to the terms of the injunction, committal to prison or payment of a fine could follow as for a contempt of court. In other words, in face of the reaction of public opinion, a prolonged conciliation procedure, with possible ultimate civil proceedings in court for an injunction, followed by a possible committal for contempt, was substituted for the criminal sanction first proposed. Though I personally had some responsibility for preparing the original scheme, in retrospect I think if we had persisted with the criminal penalty we would have made a mistake. The public would not I think in the long run have stomached a criminal prosecution for the kind of discriminatory behaviour it was sought to restrain. There would have been a danger of public sympathy going out in too large a measure to those charged, as one prosecution followed another.

It would have been unwise to ignore the risk, for example, that sooner or later a publican would as a matter of principle have insisted on going to prison rather than pay a fine imposed upon him; the image of the martyr would have begun to emerge and resentment grow against his supposed 'persecutors', the unfortunate people against whom he had discriminated. This is all a question of individual judgment and assessment of possible or likely public reaction; but if this assessment is right and if, worse still, ill-will to the criminal penalties had over the years grown to the point at which some government felt bound to modify or annul the relevant legislation, I can imagine no more disastrous defeat for decency and fair-play as between the different groups of citizens who compose our community. I am sure that in all the circumstances the change from a criminal penalty to processes of conciliation with the possibility of an ultimate injunction pronounced by a civil court in the event of final failure of conciliation, was right and inevitable. Here, then, was a case in which, if this change were wise, authority was most desperately anxious to achieve a highly necessary objective for the public good, namely, the heading off of the kind of conditions that might over the years give rise to resentments capable of bringing to this country its own version of the tragedy of the race-riot-torn streets of U.S. cities; and yet it was borne in on authority that, highly desirable as the social objective might be, the criminal law was not a suitable or acceptable instrument for its attainment and, indeed, that recourse to law in any form would best be avoided unless elaborate conciliation methods had first been tried and found unavailing.

This example of an unavoidable change from a criminal to a long-stop civil remedy illustrates, I think rather strikingly, the proposition that there are some things the law – notably the criminal law – just cannot do and that the law cannot always, even in very important contexts, be harnessed by authority to achieve its very necessary and proper purposes. But the question raised by this Act is still more far-reaching. There was pressure in 1965 to extend the Bill which became the Race Relations Act of 1965 to prevent discrimination in employment, the sale and letting of houses, the granting of credit and in other fields. The Government declined on the ground, broadly, that good sense and voluntary fair dealing should be allowed to play their part without legal compulsion, at any rate until experience showed, if it did show, that public intervention by legal enactment was unavoidable. I think that this refusal was wise. When the country was gradually coming to realise that it was confronted with a major new social problem in the shape of large-scale immigration from the Commonwealth, and able to discern only in dim outline the considerable dimensions of the problem, the Government would, when introducing legislation wholly novel in this country in purpose and scope, have been ill-advised, in my view, to carry it in the first stage beyond a certain point likely to be acceptable and understood by public opinion, making it, as it did, applicable to discrimination only in public places in the first instance. In commending the Bill to the House of Commons on third reading the Government spokesman (myself) said it must be left to actual experience to determine whether further extension of the Act was desirable. Experience since has shown that, despite all the efforts of people of goodwill to prevent it, ill-will and discrimination have developed and exist on a considerable scale. The Government have annoucned that they intend to extend the 1965 Act to cover discrimination in employment, housing, letting of premises, credit and insurance.*

The question arises whether the Act should now be extended in its application. On the one side, those against it rather irrelevantly, if truly, say you can't by legislation make people like each other. No, but you can by law make them, within limits, refrain from certain sorts of conduct towards each other. On the other side, some say, 'It's time the Race Relations Act were given teeth to bite with.' It is so easy to use glib language of this sort; but it is worse than useless to give the Act false teeth that won't chew properly. Legislation of this kind exists in some countries. Would it succeed in present and foreseeable circumstances in our own? Would it, as of course is profoundly to be hoped, prevent the emergence of a status of second class citizen, employed only in the worst employments when employed at all, housed and herded together only in soulless, overcrowded ghettos, the nightmare of two mutually antagonistic nations of two colours in England's green and pleasant land? It is a hundred per cent justified if it would help to avoid such a disaster overtaking this country, overwhelming it with sorrows and hatreds for decades to come. Or would such legislation, as some argue, serve rather to exasperate and inflame just those very dislikes and prejudices it is designed to allay – affording yet one more rather melancholy example of the cases in which the law is comparatively impotent to help in the achievement of a social objective which all want to achieve.

It is perhaps in a very broad sense accurate to say that in

* This was written before the Race Relations Act 1968 became available.

general the primary (though not the only) and direct object which gave rise to the Race Relations Act 1965 was the maintenance of public order. Its major immediate purpose was to enlarge and improve upon the Public Order Act 1936, a somewhat different and much more drastic approach being employed: (a) by the prohibition of incitement to race hatred as such, without there being any requirement (as there is in the Public Order Act 1936) to prove a likelihood of a breach of the peace as the result of the incitement; (b) by the provisions to prevent discrimination in public places as defined in the Act against persons on the ground of their colour, racial, ethnic or national origin.

But to regard the 1965 Act as having only this purpose is to miss a great deal of its real and longer-term significance. It was essential to maintain order and prevent disorderly expressions of hostility and prejudice and the deliberate fomentation of such feelings as a first step. But, in a sense more important, the Race Relations Act 1965 was designed to be only the first stage of a really comprehensive attempt at the adjustment of relationships between the different racial groups in this country, to be followed by other steps if and when experience showed they were necessary which, it was hoped, they would not be. The 1965 Act was intended to point the way to the future in a completely new area of legislation, brought into being by a wholly new social situation – that is to say, if experience of the development of this social situation showed that the position could not safely be left as it was with the 1965 Act. It was meant to feel the way.

The question now posed is whether a major further step should be undertaken by an attempt in effect to remodel social relationships by the use of law. Has the time come to cross the Rubicon and, if so, in what strength? Few would, I believe, deny that if and to the extent that the law is really an apt instrument to use, in this context of social relationships, it should be used.

How far will legislation to extend the Race Relations Act 1965 to prevent discrimination in employment, housing, insurance and credit succeed? This is a massive extension. How far would it prove to be enforceable and achieve its objective?

I

'Success' is a relative concept – would such legislation prove enforceable to a considerable extent over a long period of time?

There are, I think, three strong reasons which justify confidence that such legislation would be successful:

1. *Its timing.* I have said earlier that I think it would have been unwise in 1965 to extend the scope of the Race Relations Act 1965. Public opinion was far from ready for it and was far from convinced that such extended legislation was necessary. It had no experience of legislation of that type. The British people were far from conscious then that they were in the presence of a new and serious social problem. Legislation of that type, substantially entrenching, as it must, of its nature, on the area of private choice, would, I believe, have been strongly resented and not understood. The position is, I think, now quite changed. The people of this country have the American experience before their eyes. The consequences of inaction and neglect of the problem are plain to be seen. There has been and still is in process the fullest public discussion of 'discrimination', 'the status of second class citizens', 'race antagonisms' and all the moral and social issues involved. The British people are possibly sometimes a little slow to reconcile themselves to the fact that they are face to face with a potentially critical situation. But as their history shows it is the great quality of their genius that, once the noise and shouting have died down, they accept that they must react to such a situation and, discarding panic and hysteria, coolly and calmly get down round the table of broad and orderly public debate through all the appropriate organs of Parliament, public platform and press and work out practical, commonsense solutions. Now that they are convinced by the plain facts of today's situation, as I believe they are, that matters cannot be allowed to drift, they will, I believe, address themselves to their task with the same discipline, commonsense, compromise and tolerance that has over the centuries enabled them to lead the world in the science of social and political evolution.

2. *Reverence for the rule of law.* This is very deeply engrained in the British character. Iconoclasts may cavil and chaff at cherished and time-honoured forms, usages and principles of our democracy and constitution, begotten of centuries of con-

flict and unbroken experience, at the deep public respect for the profession and practice of the law, at the semi-sanctity that surrounds judicial office, at expressions like 'the Mother of Parliaments' and 'the British sense of fair play'. Yet all these things have bred in the British people an instinct and a readiness to obey the law, because it is the law, beyond that of other peoples. A proposed enactment which has run the full gauntlet of fierce and relentless public and Parliamentary criticism in its passage from the minister's desk and the draftsman's pen to the ultimate sanctuary of the written word of the Statute Book is happily invested with almost holy reverence by the public conscience in this country, which makes possible the achievement of lawful behaviour within its terms, however irksome they may appear, provided they are recognised as fundamentally fair, which might be wholly beyond the patience and powers of self-restraint of other nations.

3. *The legislation would, in principle, be regarded as fundamentally fair.* Although there may be some who would argue that first generation coloured immigrants, unlike the enslaved forebears of the coloured population of the United States, came here of their own accord and accordingly, as previous streams of immigrants to this country, should as it were take pot luck, such arguments could not possibly with the least semblance of fairness be used of the second generation children born in this country, and the first generation slips easily and quickly into the second. Even the most prejudiced cannot gainsay that there is something grossly unfair and abhorrent in putting a child or grown-up at a constant disadvantage because of something – their colour – which they cannot possibly help. Though they may no longer be able to dominate by their wealth and armed strength the British people will, I think, gain an ascendancy over the many other nations faced with similar problems by the example they show in the prudence and humanity with which they are seen in the coming years to face up to this difficult challenge in social adjustment.

Different aspects of the legislation may of course produce more or less useful results and be more or less successful. My own belief is that anti-discrimination provisions in the field of employment are by far the most important and, provided they do not trench too far upon personal, intimate or confidential employer-employee relationships likely to produce by far the most useful results. I think it important, in order to make such provisions workable and fully effective, that the general frame-work of a process of conciliation on the broad lines set out in the Race Relations Act 1965 in the first place, perhaps with some variations, and only a long-stop recourse to a civil court in the event of a failure at efforts of conciliation, should be retained.

Even if, in the short-term, such legislation in the field of employment may stir some resentments, in the longer term when we have grown used to it and come to regard it as part of the normal pattern of our legislation, it would, I think, go a very long way to preventing the clashes and antagonisms which otherwise might lead to the reproduction in England of the present day American scene. Discrimination in employment would I think in general be not too difficult to prove in court should that be necessary and the law would be enforceable. My guess and hope would be that in any event it would only be on rare occasions that it would be necessary to have recourse to the courts for any remedies provided to end discrimination in employment. Once the legislation was understood, its mere presence on the statute book would I think be sufficient in the majority of cases to prevent discrimination, where otherwise it might have occurred. Moreover, when people enjoy good incomes many of the other social problems tend to resolve them-selves, such as the herding together of too many in bad, over-crowded housing conditions in ghetto areas.

But my conjecture would be that there might be more difficulty in framing anti-discrimination legislation in the field of housing and, to a somewhat less extent, insurance and credit which was acceptable as being not too restrictive of private choice on the one hand and not too easy to evade owing to its provisions being too moderate on the other. Legislation against discrimination in the sale of houses on a housing estate developed on a large scale by a property developer or by a local authority should be easier to frame as to be enforceable. But in the case of sales of houses or the granting of leases of flats by individual owners of property, there may be more difficulties to deal with in drafting appropriate legislation. The eternal dilemma presents itself – such legislation might be so framed as to be easy to dodge by excuses that the refusal to accept the coloured applicant was really not attributable to his colour but to some other reason; or, on the other hand, in order to prevent this sort of evasion, such might be the sternness of its provisions, designed to frustrate such excuses, that reasonable people might be shocked at it and not hesitate to defy it and encourage others to do so. To take a purely random example, a timorous elderly would-be lessor has untruthfully said to a would-be coloured lessee that there is no vacancy, the real reason for the refusal being not that he or she refused to accept coloured people as such, but, for example, that he or she had just read in the newspapers a widely publicised court case of coloured people trafficking in drugs; with the result that the would-be lessor is genuinely fearful lest, if he or she let to a coloured person, there might be trouble over drug-taking on the premises. (I am not for a moment suggesting that coloured people are worse offenders in this regard than white people.) Should or should not the law be so framed as in such a case to compel the lessor to let to a coloured person? If not, it would surely be easy to evade the law – if yes, the law might seem harsh. Such instances might be multiplied almost ad infinitum. The dilemma would, I imagine, constantly present itself. It must be for the art and wisdom of the lawmaker to steer a safe course between Scylla and Charybdis, drafting his law neither in such lenient terms as to fail in large measure of its purpose, declining into little more than legal window-dressing, and becoming little more in course of time than a rather squalid sop to a sleepy social conscience, lulled into uneasy slumber until suddenly the trumpets of serious social disorder rudely awakened it, nor in terms that trench so roughly on the sphere of private choice that it provokes resistance and refusal to conform.

I merely seek to pose questions which seem to me to require consideration on the purely legal implications of the matter. In the sphere of anti-discrimination legislation there will be found, I am sure, rich and valuable experience of just what the law can do and cannot do to achieve the will of authority. Time will tell; but the problem of Commonwealth immigration is clearly not one which authority can rely upon the law alone to solve. In this area the law can be no more than the comparatively lowly handmaiden to a prodigious and spontaneous effort of goodwill on the part of millions of citizens of all colours – goodwill not for a short time only, but over a very long period, in spite of disappointment and setback, patient of difficulties and obstinately refusing to be disillusioned even by the ugliest and most repeated manifestations of human unreason, unconcern, and callousness. It is, after all, one of the great problems of population adjustment which the onward flow of the current of history is bound from century to century to bring to the surface and which has to be met first and foremost by a voluntary effort of humanity and a firm purpose to adapt our thinking and national attitudes to an epoch in which few, if any, nations can expect to remain in the long term other than multi-racial on a considerable scale.

But there is a converse to this which I believe is equally true. If the law can be no more than the handmaiden to goodwill, she is a handmaiden with whose services goodwill cannot dispense. Voluntary goodwill will, I think, be from time to time obstructed by oppositions, jealousies and prejudices which will frustrate its endeavour unless there are legal sanctions to which recourse may be had from time to time in case of need to overcome such obstruction. Goodwill by itself is not enough unless supported and buttressed by the law.

I stressed above that we are a very law-abiding people and that we could make this kind of law work even if other nations are much less successful in doing so. Whilst this is an immense advantage there is an obverse side – in a sense it could be a disadvantage. It is an advantage in that if the law enacted is so framed as to be workable, the British public, once they have understood and accepted its purpose, can be relied on to do their level best to comply with it and try to make it work. Conversely, if unhappily experience shows that it is not acceptable, perhaps because unwisely framed, and sensible people just won't have it and don't find their consciences strained by resistance to it and defiance, so that it simply cannot be enforced, then in due course I am sure it would have to come off the Statute Book or be curtailed in its scope. It may be that in some countries major legislation of this kind could remain as a dead-letter on the statute book and be treated by general assent as not enforceable and something about which nobody need bother, not even to the extent of repealing it or curtailing it. But I believe that in this country respect for the law is too deep-rooted in people's minds for such a situation to be tolerated. It would, of course, be an exaggeration to say that there has never been allowed to remain on the statute book a law more honoured in the breach than in the observance. But in the case of laws of such great importance as a new act to deal with race relations, should it not work as hoped, there could in my view be no question of it remaining inoperative on the Statute Book. Public controversy would soon arise; and some government would inevitably be obliged to remove it or drastically restrict its scope on a scale which would permit of its enforcement in perhaps a very modified form, probably falling far short of anything adequate to make a real impact on the social problem. Such a withdrawal or modification of the Act, should it become inevitable, would constitute a clear recognition that the law is powerless in these matters beyond a certain point and a bitter reverse to the hopes of those many people who rely on enlightened law as an instrument with which to grapple with the evil of race discrimination. Any apparent connivance by the authorities and people at large on a considerable scale at some tolerated half or quarter enforcement of a fundamental statute of this kind would, I feel sure, impart a great shock to the public conscience and gravely undermine confidence in and respect for the law – an evil result comparable in its long-term bad effects with the social evil itself it was designed to combat. Such legislation must be either fully or substantially effective or it must go. The repeal or drastic curtailment of such legislation because it could not be enforced would, I think, be such a disaster that it simply must not be allowed to happen. The utmost care and foresight must be used (as I am sure it will) so to formulate the legislation as entirely to obviate the risk of its happening. At least the Government will not be sailing in unchartered seas. It will have, to guide it, the experience of other countries, notably the

United States, and be spurred by the certain knowledge that all this threatens to be not merely a British or American problem but that race conflict, if not appeased, could in the coming years disfigure the world.

May I sum up and then conclude with a major qualification to my treatment up to this point of the title given to me, 'Authority and the Law'? My theme is that 'authority', in the sense I have defined it, society, call it what you please, determines in a broad sense that certain general objectives are desirable of attainment – such as social justice, good order, general happiness and prosperity. It then begins to fall at loggerheads within itself when it tries to relate these broad objectives to the actual circumstances of practical, daily life. Its broad unanimity of purpose gives place to a raucous discord of individual wills which is given such coherence as can be achieved by the processes of Parliament, the press and public controversy churning out practical decisions as to what is to be done in a given state of circumstances. There is no real difficulty in framing all those decisions when necessary in precise legal language and concept. But the sanction behind the legislation which emerges must rest and depend on its broad acceptance as reasonable and appropriate by the general mass of reasonable and honest-minded people, whether citizens in a community or member nations in a world community of nations. There is a *ne plus ultra* beyond which it is unwise and, indeed, impossible to enforce the will of authority, even if discernible, by the enactment of laws. I have tried to sketch out some examples and situations in which these limitations seem to appear. Pressed beyond that point the law, particularly the criminal law, may become impotent and even recoil upon those who promulgate it.

'So what?' the reader may ask. 'Are you arguing that people won't obey laws they do not like and that therefore the rule of law, domestically and internationally, is little more than a pipedream?' Most certainly not; so long as it is understood that the 'rule of law' is a relative expression. In a vast sphere of behaviour, as individuals and communities, we comply with the law and there are legal sanctions adequate to compel us to do so if of our own free will we were not prepared to comply. But the lawmaker must be on his guard against overstraining the law, addressing it to tasks it cannot accomplish. It is comparatively easy to put it on the Statute Book. But, once there, it will run the gauntlet of public scrutiny and criticism in its application, in practice, to the countless different actual situations with which the life of a community will present it, often in an atmosphere of ill-will, prejudice, sympathy for the individuals against whom it operates, misunderstanding or inaccurate understanding of its effects and objectives. Unless it is so thought out in advance by those who enact it as to be able to stand this test, it had better not be put on the statute book at all. It can only work with broad public sympathy and support behind it and the building up of this support and understanding is the function and result of general education, based on experience and discussion, through all the public organs available for that purpose. In the long run it is goodwill and good sense by which we must govern ourselves rather than by good law which can function effectively only in so far as it is the expression of goodwill and good sense. Idealism is a sacred flame without which life is brutish. But we are, in general, in disposition and character rather good, not very good; in some things selfish, in some things unselfish. We won't in general conform to ideal standards, except perhaps in a period of danger and crisis until it is over. Lawmakers. must recognise this. It is one aspect of saying that politics is the art of the possible. So long as the law does not expect too much of us we obey it. Beyond this point it is often not a serviceable instrument for authority to use to enforce its will.

My qualification is as follows: to point only to limitations, as I have done hitherto, to the efficiency of law as an instrument of policy and leave it at that would be to convey an impression grotesquely misleading and incomplete. Side by side with its limitations must be set the myriad human relationships which are effectively subject to the rule of law. The whole body of the law of tort, contract, equity, crime, social law, law safeguarding personal liberty, constitutional law and law in many other areas, domestic, foreign and international, constitute a gigantic corpus of rules which guide and regulate almost every aspect of our individual and group conduct. Sometimes this is so even in matters which the law does not touch; because the law has acquired a general respect based on a mystique. Simple people the world over, particularly in English-speaking countries, and countries influenced by their thinking, use phrases like, 'It is against the law', or, 'I claim my rights under the law', not knowing to what law they are referring, or, if there is one applicable, what are its terms, and very often where there is, in fact, no law applicable. Who, for example, could state with precision what in law constitutes such a widely known type of misbehaviour as 'theft'? At the time these lines are written Parliament is engaged on a massive overhaul of the whole concept and formulation of the crime of theft; because the existing definition in the Larceny Act 1916 has been found to be unsatisfactory and uncertain. In the minds of millions of people who are not lawyers, law has become almost identified with good conduct – they think the wisdom of law all-pervading. So omniscient is it that surely it must provide an answer in every difficult dilemma of conduct. Without it must be anarchy, oppression, misery; and the temptation to dwell on its imperfections springs often from a deep feeling that it is something of inestimable value that almost approaches perfection.

It is because of my respect for it that I have perhaps yielded too much to this temptation in what I have written above – perhaps also because through long personal contact with it and affection for it I hate to think of it as bruised, broken, humiliated. At any rate, on this qualification of what I have said, I close; and by making this quaification seek to redress the balance as I think it should be.

General Sir John Hackett, G.C.B., C.B.E., D.S.O., M.C., A.D.C.

Commander-in-Chief, British Army of the Rhine
Commander, Northern Army Group, NATO

The author writes towards the end of a long period of regular service in the British Army. The views expressed here, however, are entirely his own. When he speaks of 'the military' he is thinking mostly of the British Army of today. Nevertheless, much of what he has to say may be generally true of military service as a whole and in particular of service in the Royal Navy and the Royal Air Force. The term 'soldier' is used largely for convenience. It is hoped that sailors and airmen will take no offence at this and apply only as much of what is said here of soldiers to their own Services as they feel inclined.

Of all enterprises undertaken by groups of men the military stands out probably more clearly than any as demanding authoritative direction. The function of critical importance in it is the conduct of battle. The pressures and uncertainties of battle are very great. The rewards of success can be high, the penalties for failure, not only for the military group itself but also for the bigger social groupings in whose interests it operates, catastrophic. In battle response has to be swift. Resolution and ruthlessness must be marked. Moreover, since in most critical command decisions in battle judgment is inevitably more intuitive than reasoned, these decisions tend to come from a single person. Military authority is in essence autocratic.

Policy direction can be formulated in a group, for example,

140

---

by a committee. In exceptional circumstances what is clearly recognisable as a military command decision can also be made by a group but this is comparatively rare. It happens more readily where grouping is random than where it is institutionalised and more readily in smaller groups than in larger. It happens most readily of all, perhaps, when the members of a small group are themselves the executants of the group's command decisions. Small parties of escapers moving through the enemy's territory have been known to conduct their affairs in this way, that is, by agreement between themselves. Even then one member of the party may, for one reason or another (force of personality, perhaps, or the persistence of an earlier relationship) be accepted as final arbiter.

The larger the political component in the process of making decisions the more nearly we approach what can be called command by committee. The level at which something of this sort is not only desirable but unavoidable has been depressed in recent times by increase in the complexity of warlike operations. Control by a single individual of proliferating agencies – and even their full comprehension – has grown more and more difficult. As you go down the scale of subordination towards what soldiers call the sharp end, however, a point is inevitably reached at which a single commander is responsible and the decisions taken must be his. Military command remains, in essence, autocratic.

Very little of the military man's lifetime will be spent in battle. The overwhelming majority of military men go through life without, as they put it, hearing a shot fired in anger. The basic military situation, nonetheless, remains that of combat. The value of a military force for any purpose at all is to be judged primarily upon its capability to apply physical force in battle. What Foch said of the rearguard, that its importance lay more in being than in doing, is true of all military forces. They are important not so much for what they do as for what they can do. What they can do, more or less well, is to apply force in battle. The degree to which they can do this is the measure of their value.

Command decisions in combat are therefore the critical military decisions. They will in great part depend upon decisions taken earlier. These will already have largely determined the size, structure, composition, method and equipment of the military forces at the commander's disposal. Some decisions, particularly those relating to equipment, will have been taken long before. The general effect of these pre-combat decisions will be to limit the range of options open to the field commander in the battle. They may even have already excluded the only decisions which could bring success. The commander's skill will then be applied to the minimisation of failure. In any case command decisions will be criticial.

They are not, of course, always made by the commander, particularly at high echelons of command. The evaluation and presentation of the material upon which a decision must be based – which is the work of the staff – may here again leave a commander with little choice. In some armies, where high command has not always been allotted on grounds of professional excellence alone, it has been common for a Chief of Staff to act as the effective decision maker. This practice has at times been welcomed, not only within armies, but also outside them in the society they serve, as a safeguard against the incompetence of generals who owe their appointment to other than professional reasons. Even in extreme cases, however, the orders are authenticated by the commander. They are issued on his responsibility and in his name. The principle of the commander's unique responsibility remains unimpaired.

The commander's unique responsibility, however, does not mean that he has absolute power. His decisions are made in a closely delineated area. The authority he exercises may be great but it is highly regulated, both by ordinance and by accepted canons of practice. An officer today may post a man where he is quite likely to be killed but he may not strike him.

He may deprive him of his life but not, except as directed by the Service, of his pay.*

This was not always so. In a primitive stage of development military authority can be regarded not only as autocratic but also as virtually absolute. It was only at later stages that the powers of a military commander became both more highly regulated and more narrowly restricted, with the development of armed forces as institutions.

Physical sanctions, in early stages, played an important (though not an exclusive) part in securing obedience to authority. Fear of severe physical punishment, or of death, or even of physical punishment so drastic and prolonged that death followed, was a basic element in the maintenance of military discipline until well beyond what is called the Age of Enlightenment. In the late eighteenth century it was said with some reason that men were encouraged to be more frightened of their officers than of the enemy.

It will not do to blame the military of an earlier period for practices that we should regard as intolerable today. An army reflects the manners, as well as the social articulation, of the society from which it is raised. Brutal flogging of soldiers was nothing out of the ordinary at a time when the tormenting of lunatics or the hanging of children for trivial offences were regarded as legitimate forms of public entertainment. Manners have grown milder in our society and disciplinary practices in our armed forces have become less harsh. The dominance of those in authority has depended less and less upon physical punishment. Command has come to be exercised less by dominance of any sort than by persuasion. Even in the last resort, when obedience to the orders given will almost certainly lead to the destruction of those carrying them out, it cannot now be seriously claimed that compliance depends entirely on compulsion, under fear of punishment as the alternative.

* But outlooks change. In the Royal Navy of the mid-nineteenth century sailors were beaten but officers were not. In the Royal Navy of the mid-twentieth century sailors were no longer beaten. To lay a finger upon any of them would invite wide disapprobation and severe disciplinary action. Officers, however, were now beaten instead. Not all officers, of course, only midshipmen.

Coercion persists but its significance in the effective exercise of command can be overestimated. Its importance lies more in the prior development of a habit of obedience than in the enforcement of obedience upon the battlefield.

Just as physical sanctions are no longer fundamental to the maintenance of military authority, so outstanding qualities of physique are no longer essential to the military commander. At a very early stage brute strength not only helped to ensure the obedience to the stronger of those upon his own side. It also made of him a leader acceptable to them in war by reason of his power to afflict the opposition. Guile was also important, as Homer showed, and was certainly respected. It can be accepted, however, that in the primitive fighting group physical prowess was the most important attribute in the leader.

Everyone had a common interest in success. The defeated in battle died, either during it or, in all probability, soon afterwards. Only victory in the battle could ensure the survival of those participating in it and these accordingly found themselves inevitably bound in subordination to the person best calculated to ensure success.

In military affairs today subordination depends upon more subtle and complex factors. The basic leadership situation remains one in which a group of men require direction in an enterprise whose success is important to them all. A group of men struggling to survive in a desert will value highly the services of the man who can guide them to the waterhole. He has knowledge which they have not and is prepared to apply it so that all survive. The possession of this special knowledge, however, makes no more of him than a guide unless he can furnish something more. At this point the question of management begins to emerge, not only in its more or less mechanical aspect of organisation but in the probably more important matter of helping people over difficulties. In military management the exercise of authority is a necessary (though not the only) element.

In a military group the man in authority is distinguished by a rank, in virtue of which those of lesser rank are expected to accept his direction. It must be said at once, however, that rank in and for itself is an incomplete reason for the acceptance of subordination by fighting men, no matter how highly institutionalised the enterprise may be. An armed force may quite readily coast along upon its rank structure in time of peace. Subordination which depends upon forms of rank alone may prove too frail to withstand the stresses of war. Military authority may be buttressed by forms of all sorts. It cannot be wholly effective unless much more is at the disposal of its holder than simply the badges of rank upon his coat.

Although this is not the place for a full analysis of the characteristics required of the military leader, it would be inappropriate not to remark upon at least some of them. First of all professional skill has come to be indispensable.

The span of technical skills now required in military operations has broadened at a tremendous rate since the industrial revolution. Even as late as the mid-eighteenth century a field commander could still be a master of most, if not all, of the more important skills practised by those under his command. The Maréchal de Saxe was perhaps one of the last high commanders of land forces of whom it could be said that he was. This has ceased to be possible now for a very long time.

Nevertheless, a military commander must be seen to possess in high degree some, at least, of the specific skills applied by those below him and must be capable at the same time of applying the whole complex of skills, including those he has not mastered, to the desired end. He is thus required to possess in the military sphere both specific skills and a general managerial capability. Without the first he is unlikely to secure the confidence of the specialists below him. Without the second he is unlikely to be able to direct the common enterprise to success. He can readily be given the confidence of those whose speciality is in something else, provided that his own is relevant. Thus an infantry division can happily accept command by a general who is basically an officer of artillery. But the commander who is not recognised as possessing in satisfactory degree some relevant skill is unlikely to receive that degree of

K

confidence without which no amount of managerial capability will suffice.

A second skill in which the military leader must demonstate proficiency is in the management of fear. This is a skill not uniquely demanded in the military profession but it is of very high importance there. Unless the leader in battle is able to demonstrate that his own ability to manage fear is at least as great as that generally to be found in those under his command his authority may be difficult to sustain. This is particularly important at lower levels of command, where the leader and the led are associated in a dangerous environment which brings them very closely together.

A reputation for courage will pursue an officer from lower levels of command to higher, though bravery may here be less frequently required. Even then occasions are likely to arise in which he will be expected to face very considerable (and probably sudden) physical danger. If he is now found wanting he may prove to have forfeited a considerable degree of his authority.

In a battle the example of officers is the keystone of morale. Lord Moran, in that wise and compassionate book, *The Anatomy of Courage*, refers to 'the electrifying effect of an act of coolness and courage on the part of an officer'.

A great part of this effect is, I believe, due to a sudden surge of relief in those who are witnesses. They are helped to shed a part at least of the intolerable burden of inadequacy under which they labour. They see another man doing what they long to do and cannot, someone being what they long to be and are not. Hope and purpose are shown to them where they labour in futility and despair and a rush of gratitude and humility and love can be the result. There is something here of Redemption.

To these two skills I add one more. Unlike the second, which has to do with managing oneself, this concerns itself more with the handling of others.

What makes men, once embarked on military service, continue to accept the authority of a military superior? The simplest answer is that from the earliest days of regular armies a soldier, often brought into service by force or deception, or because he saw absolutely no alternative, was kept there by the threat of harsh punishment if he tried to leave before his employers wanted him to. It is still said that men sometimes join the Services under a misapprehension and only discover their mistake when, in the terms of a contract carrying penal sanctions, it is too late to leave.

All this is too simple. If this were all there were to it soldiers brought into battle would shoot their own officers first, not in the occasional exception but as a matter of routine. Whatever practices may have been responsible in earlier days for the procurement of men into military service, and however heavily the fear of punishment may have borne upon them, I find it hard to believe that Alexander the Great could have taken an army from Attica to the Indus under the whip alone, or that the bloody backs of British redcoats in the eighteenth century were the sole, or even the principal, reasons for the impeccable behaviour of British infantry at Minden.

The Maréchal de Saxe wrote that what governs the behaviour of men in battle 'lies in human hearts and one should search for it there. It is in the human heart that the reasons should be sought for the greater or less success of armies.' This matter, he says, 'is the most important, the most learned and the most profound of the profession of war. Without a knowledge of the human heart one is dependent upon the favour of fortune, which is sometimes very inconsistent.' Our knowledge of the human heart, he added, is far from perfect.

Oliver Cromwell in the English Civil War, a battlefield commander probably two centuries ahead of his time, was almost certainly only able to apply his advanced methods by what Clarendon called his 'wonderful understanding of the natures and humour of men'.

Military command in its essence, that is to say, in the successful direction of men in battle, is and always has been of a highly manipulative nature. The material nowadays is possibly in some respects different from what it was when Wellington contemplated 'that article' out of his window in Brussels and told Creevey that success in the critical battle ahead all depended on how many of him would be available. But if the material has changed it must still be manipulated. What is different is probably the points at which and the methods by which you can best handle it.

One such method is to create within the military force a continuous vertical structure of confidence from top to bottom. Military commanders, as a matter of highest priority, set about developing this as well as they are able. Some are better at it than others. All try to improve the vertical communication structure in the forces under their command.

First hand personal acquaintance is here essential. A land force commander in modern conditions, which demand a very high degree of dispersal, must spend a great deal of time and undergo much personal inconvenience to get to know, and make himself known to, the troops under his command.

In a naval vessel what almost seems to be the opposite happens. The Captain and the ship's company are continuously housed in close contiguity. Considerable attention must here be given to ensuring that the man in authority is kept apart to an appropriate degree from the men under his command.

The successful exercise of command demands a very considerable degree of personal acquaintance between different levels. It also requires the preservation of a certain degree of detachment on the part of the man in authority.

At different levels of command qualities sometimes seem to be required which differ not only in degree but in kind from those required elsewhere. 'I have known very good colonels', says the Maréchal de Saxe, 'become very bad generals.' Liddell-Hart in his memoirs suggests that the reverse may also be true. He refers to one of Britain's most successful commanders in World War II as an outstanding example of how 'born commanders' can be surpassed by a 'made commander'. This particular officer, according to Liddell-Hart, 'did not show the natural signs of leadership, or a knack of handling men – indeed, when he was eventually given command of a battalion, after sixteen years on the staff, he brought it to the verge of mutiny by misjudged handling'. The officer in question turned out later to be a very successful commander of an Army Group.

So far I have been discussing the nature of military authority and some of the factors which help to create and maintain it. It is perhaps now worth considering to what end this authority may be exercised and what is implied in its exercise for the commander concerned.

The function of a military commander, though much of what he has to do in battle is destructive, is nevertheless essentially constructive and positive. His business is to impose upon the disorderly substance of a battle an order of his own choosing His work has close affinities with that of the artist, whose business is the same – to reduce to an order of his own choice the material upon which he works.

Devoted to the bringing about in battle of a situation ordered upon acceptable lines, a military man lives a life which is itself orderly. He accepts authority and exercises it in a framework which may have imperfections but is at its best highly efficient. The military man not only operates inside this framework. He very largely lives within it. In his work and way of life he is relieved of many uncertainties. He can locate himself. He knows not only what he is, but where. He knows his place, his duties, his responsibilities to those above, below and on either side of him. He knows his rights and also his privileges. He can identify the location of other members of the same institution and the relationship of their loci to each other and to his own.

The military man has to recognise his own place in the military command structure. This not only means that he must be prepared to accept all the responsibilities of his own level of command, taking the load and giving the decisions expected of him. It also means that he must be prepared loyally to accept his own position of subordination to the levels of command above. 'I am a man under authority,' said the centurion, 'having soldiers under me.' Authority in the military institution seems only possible in a state of subordination to yet higher authority. It is certainly to us in Britain inconceivable for a military person to have soldiers set under him unless he too is subordinate.

To some the idea of the ordered life could be repugnant. It might represent, perhaps, an invasion of personal liberty which would be intolerable. The man who accepts it, however, usually finds that the regulation of a large part of his life does not have a generally restrictive effect. The result may be quite the reverse.*

There are things you cannot do in the armed services. Very well: you cannot do them. It is convenient in many cases to be spared the onus of decision and a possible difficulty in choice.

The ordered way of life may not have to be accepted. It may even be sought. In troubled centuries men sometimes looked for protection in monastic orders and found there liberation from a host of other cares. Military service can offer something of the same kind.

De Vigny, a former professional soldier himself who never lost his affectionate interest in the military, was always impressed by the placid and dignified demeanour commonly displayed by professional soldiers. He believed he had found the reason for it in resignation. But 'resignation' implies the existence of factors you would change if you could. It is only if you cannot escape them that you must make the best of it and endure what you cannot change.

I do not believe that the military life of today requires resignation to make it tolerable. To fret not in a narrow convent cell may be possible only for someone inclined to be a nun. But to someone so inclined the restrictions of this life may not demand anything that can be called resignation. What is required is no more than acceptance. When the limitations are accepted a feeling of liberation can result.†

---

* I recently suggested to a well-known journalist that there were advantages in being spared, as the soldier is, the need for many decisions on unimportant matters – like the choice of a tie to wear to work, for example. He protested that choosing a tie was typical of those small expressions of free-will which contribute to the aggregate of human liberty. Deprivation of the right and duty to make these would be intolerable.

Yet my companion was one of those who enthusiastically support an increasing degree of public regulation in highly important areas of private interest. Let the State tell me, he seemed to say, how, where or by whom my children shall be educated so long as I am allowed to choose my own tie! The argument here is not against State direction. It is about relative values.

† The whole question of freedom in service deserves fuller enquiry than is possible here. A general examination of this problem could well start with a study of the ethics of military subordination.

I have said something of the relationship, within the military environment, of one soldier to another. External relationships are also important. In other societies different in size, complexity and history from our own, military power can perhaps be imagined which is not subordinate in the last resort to the civil. In our own society the ultimate subordination of the military to the civil has long been regarded as not only acceptable but inevitable.

Only once since the Reformation has the Government of England been disfigured by the intrusion of exclusively military characteristics. This happened, curiously enough, at the hands of a man widely admired as a champion of popular freedom. Cromwell's rule of the major generals was short-lived, little liked and not particularly efficient. There has fortunately been nothing like it since 1660.

Today we see every year, upon the Sovereign's official birthday, massive military evolutions performed by household infantry, fighting foot-soldiery without superiors anywhere, within a stone's throw of the Cabinet offices. No one sees here a danger to civil government from the military.

Subordinate as they are to the civil in the last resort, within armed forces themselves authority proceeds downwards through the military hierarchy. When Napoleon said that to learn to command it was first necessary to learn to obey he may have been referring chiefly to the acquisition of command techniques. It is highly probable that he had in mind, in addition, the moral content of military subordination. The exercise of authority and submission to it are in the moral sphere most closely related. They are even, in a sense, one.

It has always seemed to me that officers in the Army tend to receive from those below them no more, in the long run, than they are prepared to give to those above. The loyalty they are willing to offer to superiors seems to be the measure of the loyalty they are likely to receive in their turn from subordinates.

This is not always clearly seen. Sometimes attempts are made to purchase compliance from subordinates by the affectation of a fine disregard for superiors. It is not only beginners in the exercise of command who make this mistake. Wherever it occurs

it represents short-term expediency which is in the highest
degree dangerous.

In the American Civil War, when Abraham Lincoln appointed Hooker to command the army of the Potomac he was
making the best choice he could, but he knew Hooker had
faults. He knew, for instance, that Hooker had tried to obstruct
his predecessor, Burnside. In his letter of appointment Lincoln
wrote: 'I much fear that the spirit which you have decided to
infuse into the army of criticising their commander and with-
holding confidence from him will now turn upon you.'

Civil and military are closely related. It should be clearly
recognised nonetheless that a member of the profession of arms
is not, and as such never can be, a civilian. His profession has
much in common with some others. In these the extent to which
a man is bound in the discharge of his proper function cannot
be wholly regulated by contracts between men. The priest, the
teacher, the healer, the artist, the scholar, the law-giver – and
for somewhat different reasons the farmer and the sailor – are
bound by a discipline emerging from the very nature of their
tasks. Whatever may be said in the contract the relationship
between, say, teacher and pupil or doctor and patient cannot
wholly be contained within it. The determination of what must
be done by the one for the other will at some point cease to be
possible in terms of agreements.

In the contract of the military man there lies, unwritten but
all important, what can only be described as a clause of un-
limited liability. So long as he operates under this contract he
belongs to what Windham called 'a class of men set apart from
the general mass of the community'. As a soldier he will never
cease to be a citizen. Until he ceases to be a soldier he cannot
be a civilian.

It is therefore at all levels clearly wrong to regard the military
officer as a civil servant, even when the work he does, as is often
the case at higher levels in Whitehall, is more like that of a
civil servant than what is expected of a sailor, soldier or airman.
In Britain a military officer is commissioned into the Service of
the Crown and is a servant of Government by reason of the
Crown's position as the Sovereign Head of the Executive. His

service is under arms and his function is military. It involves the application of force, with all the responsibility for the safety of others and all the personal hazard to himself which may result. A civil servant in Britain is also employed by the Crown but he is engaged under quite different terms, to assist in the discharge of the Crown's administrative function. The qualities demanded in a civil servant are different in many respects from those required in the soldier. His liability, too, is limited. Hazard to life and limb has no place in it.

There is thus, from the nature of their contracts both in the written and the unwritten clauses, a fundamental distinction between the civil servant and the soldier. This distinction is sometimes not grasped where it should be.*

I have said earlier that the function of the military commander is to impose order, and that in this he may be likened to others who do much the same. What then sets the military enterprise apart?

The existence of an objective common to all participants in it – the objective of success in the battle – distinguishes the military undertaking from, for example, the industrial. As Maréchal Lyautey pointed out in an article in the *Revue des deux Mondes* in 1891, after France had introduced universal military service, there does not exist in armies the divergence of interest which dominates industry. In industry, he argued, the entrepreneur normally directs his activities to the securing of maximum personal profit. The worker is guided chiefly by the urge to sell his labour at the highest possible price. In the basic industrial situation increased material advantage can be procured for one by increased disadvantage to the other. In armed forces in enlightened countries no member of management should be materially better off by reason of the exploitation of subordinates.

Management in industry today would certainly not accept the position in the possibly oversimplified terms in which Lyautey sets it out. Profit in the industrial operation is not the

* Mr. Frank Allaun (Member for Salford, East): '. . . a general – who is, after all, a civil servant – . . .' Hansard, Vol. 760, Tues. 5 Mar. 1968, column 305.

only incentive to efficiency, though it is an effective measure of it and one for which there is unfortunately no real substitute in armed forces. But whatever combination of motives may operate upon the industrialist in addition to the search for gain, the phrase 'the two sides of industry' is too firmly established and too widely used not to indicate a real division.

Military men leaving their Service often find trade unions strange. They usually do not at first greatly like them. The existence within the same enterprise of a divergence of interest so deep that one side apparently has to combine to resist exploitation by the other is as new in their experience as it is unwelcome.

The seamen's strike of 1966 is regarded by some as a major factor in bringing about the economic difficulties which assailed Great Britain, always sensitive on a balance of payments issue, in succeeding years. In the inexorable drift thereafter to the devaluation of the pound, and subsequent harsh measures to make devaluation work, reference has often been made to the seamen's strike as though it were an act of God. It was not: it was an act of men. One of the men chiefly responsible was reported to have said in retrospect that if the interests of the country had been the principal concern of his union he and his colleagues might well have acted differently. Since, however, their principal concern was the interests of their own members they had no alternative to what they did.

This is no place to debate the issues involved in the 1966 seamen's strike, still less to explore trade unionism in Britain. All that is relevant here is that whenever a choice of this sort arises the interest of the country is to the man in military service without any question paramount. Many die, in peace as well as in war, as a result of the total acceptance of this principle. It is scarcely surprising that when military men leave their Service they do not always feel immediately at home in a trade union environment.

Officers sometimes take a little time to realise that attitudes in the Services and in industry are very different. This is seen on resettlement courses. The working man, they have been known to say, is clearly the same sort of person that they knew in the Service. Treated in industry in the way that he was accustomed to be treated in the Service his reaction would surely be the same. Loyalty to the enterprise would result.

Those who think this way are often in for a sharp disappointment. They are sometimes even made to look a little absurd. The simple fact is that, as Lyautey pointed out, in armed service the interest of the whole enterprise is one. The interests of officers and men should not radically diverge and something is wrong when they do. There are no two sides in armed service with a requirement for formidable and elaborate machinery to reconcile them. The contract in industry is of a fundamentally different nature from the contract in service under arms.

Although the subordination of the military enterprise to political direction is accepted in the Anglo-Saxon system as indispensable the institution itself is a professional monolith. Once the point has been passed at which a political directive is handed over to the military for execution, even though political advice (and even firm instruction) may continue to be given at successive stages lower down, military authority follows the line of military responsibility. In whatever manner the military institution may be integrated into its parent society it is itself essentially hierarchic and authority within it flows from top to bottom along hierarchic lines. The officer who has not been specifically set under the orders of a non-military person – a civil administrator, let us say, a diplomat or a policeman – will expect to receive his orders from an officer above him in the hierarchy.

In the British military system authority is in considerable degree delegated. The principle is that the senior should only have to do what cannot be done by a junior. The junior is encouraged to act on his own authority. The senior accepts the blame if what is done is wrong and no doubt much of the credit for what is done well.

This, though it seems a reasonable way of doing things, is not the universal practice in other armies. In some no junior staff officer is allowed to send out anything in the name of a superior unless the document has been authenticated at a higher level.

In the British Service junior staff officers draft letters on their own initiative for the Commander-in-Chief and sign them in his name. The general pattern of the orders to be followed has been laid down from above and their practical application to detailed cases is then left to the good sense of adequately trained junior staff. I have heard it said (by a senior officer well known for his energetic pursuit of a wide range of interests) that one of the most important elements in the successful practice of high command was idleness. He would not himself wish to do, he said, anything that could possibly be done for him by anyone else.

There is truth and common sense here. Commanders who operate in this way allot tasks, objectives and means. They then leave subordinates with the minimum of interference to do what has to be done. At both levels there is greater freedom of action. The subordinates will work better and the superior can give more attention to what cannot be done by others.

Whatever the nature of authority in the military institution and however it evolves it is certainly not the product of democratic processes. It proceeds by devolution downwards from above.

In other spheres authority emerges in different ways. In the academic, for example, a considerable weight of it arises from the expression of a common will coming up from below. This is not always or universally the case. College heads are not yet appointed as a result of truly democratic election processes. Anyone who has seen policy-forming bodies in universities at work, however, would agree that a common will influences policy to an important extent.

I recall observing how sharply the processes of government found in the military system can differ from those in the academic when I was at the Royal Military College of Science at Shrivenham. The Commandant of the R.M.C.S. was a soldier, appointed to his command by the normal processes and responsible to the Department of State at the head of his Service. The academic faculty, which was of high quality, at the level of a small technological university, was entirely civilian. The Department, of course, furnished the money. It was clear that the academic faculty would work best if it were handled in the way that such a body of men would, in a university, for example, normally expect. It was also clear that if a sharp confrontation were allowed to develop between positions taken up by the faculty on the one hand and the Department on the other the faculty would be bound to lose. This could not fail to impair confidence and efficiency on the academic side. It was therefore important to prevent such a confrontation from developing. The result was a very interesting practical exercise in government, in which complete clarification of an issue might have disadvantages for the very people who sought it.

In the universities of the United Kingdom, now that in most their funds come almost entirely from the Government, and the University Grants Committee (which distributes them) must report to the Public Accounts Committee, the future holds dangers. Marked differences could emerge between what the Government, which finds the money, may find expedient and what a university, which spends it, may think right. In discussions over the fees to be paid by overseas students this has already happened. The universities will almost certainly face other conflicts of similar origin.

An army seems to need about one officer to every ten other ranks. Quite apart from the fact that an institution such as the military cannot rely upon chance for the emergence of leaders in any situation and must make sure that these are chosen, trained and appropriately located in advance, men acceptable to their fellows as leaders do not seem to be thrown up in anything like sufficient quantities by natural processes alone. An officer group has therefore become a universal feature of armed forces, distinguishable from the rest in clearly marked ways.

An officer is usually dressed differently, encouraged to keep himself somewhat apart from the members of the other group, given distinguishing badges of rank. The rules require that those beneath him in the hierarchy treat him with some degree of respect.

One reason for all this may be to cultivate otherness in the officer group in partial substitution for the betterness ideally required, since this may not be available in sufficient quantity. It is well known in armed forces that the maintenance of discipline is far more difficult where the holder of authority is constantly associated in close physical contiguity with those over whom it is exercised. This is one of the reasons for officers' messes, for sergeants' messes and for the now widespread tendency in British forces to provide even very junior NCOs with a place of their own.

The cultivation of otherness may help to explain the tendency to type-cast professional military men. Another explanation for this tendency is that military discipline is expected to produce a sameness which is assumed to exist even when it does not. Yet another is that the military profession takes very seriously a whole range of practices whose purpose, whether this is fully realised or not, is to strengthen the coherence of the military group under stress, and these tend to emphasise the military man's apartness.

Uniforms were introduced largely for ease of recognition. They later became perhaps even more important as a declaration of the unity of the military group (the regiment, for example) as a whole. Anything that increases the coherence of the military group raises its power of resistance to stress. Since military practice is essentially group practice, and the basic military situation is the battle, it is scarcely surprising that means of increasing group coherence are of high value to the military. Uniforms may be decorative, interesting, even bizarre. They also have a functional part to play. Along with other group distinctions, such as regimental differences, their contribution to the coherence of the group is unquestionably high.

Close order drills which once had tactical significance in land armies but lost it long ago are still retained for similar reasons. They are held to be useful because they develop a habit of swift response to orders. Much more important, in my own opinion, is their contribution to increased coherence in the group. Colours were once trooped so that the soldiery could be made thoroughly familiar with their appearance. Their function in the maintenance of tactical control was critical. They are trooped now as part of a ceremonial whose main value lies in developing an increased awareness of identity. The chief purpose of such activities is always the same. It is to raise resistance in the fighting group to stress.

Amongst those who deride military ceremonial it is rare indeed to find the military professional. He may not always be as articulate in defence of his practices as his critics are in the attack. But he tends to know his job. He knows that it is of paramount importance to strengthen the coherence of the group in order to increase its resistance to stress. He recognises in a distinctive style of dress, custom and behaviour, and in military ceremonial, valuable instruments to this end. They are expensive and sometimes rather a nuisance, as he well knows, but they are very useful. I would wager, on my own experience as a fighting man, that if the components in this problem could be quantified sufficiently for the ethnologists to be turned on to a study of the British regimental system they would discover it to be, not a quaint and decorative survival, but a military instrument of very high efficiency.

In Britain traditional military practice often flowers into pageantry of great beauty. This must be recognised for what it is. Beautiful though it may be, and not infrequently moving, the significance of military pageantry does not lie only in its interest as a spectacle. It is a reminder of the essential nature of the military institution, drawing attention to three of its main characteristics. These are order, apartness and unity.

Is a discontinuity unavoidable in the upward articulation of the hierarchy? Should there not be a continuous promotion path from the lowest position in armed services to the highest?

This would certainly be desirable if it were practicable. Military skills, however, take time to acquire. They are also of different sorts, of which some take longer to acquire than others. The skills required in, say, a sergeant-major of a squadron of tanks are by no means the same as the skills required of the officer commanding the squadron. But the skills of the sergeant-major, in which experience plays a very great part, are likely to take longer to learn than those of the squadron commander under whom he serves. On the other hand, the latter's skills can only be acquired on a considerable educational background.

Command in battle makes enormous demands on personal resilience and on other resources which tend to decline with increasing age. In choosing material for further promotion above, say, the rank of the officer commanding a sub-unit you must make sure that the material still has sufficient wear in it. Otherwise higher commanders may turn out to be much too old to accept the strains likely to be put upon them in war.

The comparatively early age of retirement of Service officers, which often causes comment, is an inevitable result of the search for officers young enough to carry the responsibilities of their ranks in war. A judge may be at his best beyond the age of sixty, with years of valuable service still before him. A major general commanding a division in the battle would normally, at sixty, be too old. In peacetime, when the institutional aspects of an armed service become more demanding than they do in war, ages tend to creep up. The average age, in 1968, of brigadiers on first appointment to a brigade was forty-five and a half. In the equivalent ranks of post list captain and air commodore in the sister services the relevant ages were forty-six and forty-five. By the end of World War II it was quite common for officers to be holding commands in these ranks at the age of thirty.

It will thus be seen that though the situation differs in the three British Services there would be very real difficulties in trying to set up in every one of them a complete rank continuum. Social developments in the future may allow of more successful efforts. For the time being, however, and for as far ahead as we can reasonably plan, it seems that the present discontinuities in the career structure of officers and non-officers are likely to persist. At the same time, higher management in British armed forces is very fully aware of the need to bridge over these discontinuities wherever this can be done. The possibilities of a career in commissioned rank now open to a young man, even when circumstances have resulted in his joining a Service in a non-officer stream, have very greatly increased over recent years and it is gratifying to note that they continue to be enlarged.

The urge to survive helps to account for the readiness with

which in primitive societies military authority, which guaranteed the continuance of life, has been recognised as of more importance than civil – if at an early stage such a distinction is possible – which merely ordered it. Even today, whenever the existence of a society is at stake all other requirements tend to become subordinate. Hence the ease with which abnormal administrative arrangements – emergency legislation, military government, martial law, even military dictatorship – are accepted in times of crisis, however greatly these abnormalities may diminish civil liberty. When people believe that life itself is threatened, whether it is in fact or not, they will usually be prepared to relinquish a very high degree of liberty if they believe that this will help to preserve it.

In most primitive societies a threat to survival from hostile human agencies could almost be regarded as a constant. The subordination of what we should now call civil institutions to military was then unquestioned. The warrior-king (often priest, too, for reasons that we need not now examine) was a common type. Sometimes the situation was institutionalised. Sparta offers an outstanding example. The Western European feudal system offers one no less important.

In more advanced societies safety from external dominance by force has often been the chief condition of advancement. The splendour at their prime of British parliamentary institutions, like the stable relationship that has developed in Britain between military and civil, owes much to the existence around this island of a stretch of silver sea.

The identification of personal safety for the individual (and his family) with the success of the leader in battle helped to account for a strong and persistent personal link in the feudal command system. It led easily to the acceptance of a position of natural superiority for the man who was best able to furnish military leadership.

It would be oversimplifying a complex situation to suggest that the military structure of a feudal society was based upon nothing but the ownership and tenancy of land. Nonetheless, in Western Europe, in the Middle Ages, those who through ownership or for other reasons disposed of significant areas of land were almost inevitably looked to for military leadership.

L

Land was the commonest form of wealth. Its distribution was therefore the most commonly found method of procuring military service. The introduction of the stirrup and the consequent development of armoured combat techniques based on the horse, which resulted in the dominance of Western European battlefields by the mounted man at arms for some five hundred years, placed a further premium on it. The arms, equipment and horse of a mounted warrior in twelfth century France or Germany might absorb in capital cost the income for some years of a considerable little agricultural community. The man whose resources were small, who was therefore relatively lightly armed and went on foot, inevitably became the subordinate. The man who was able to fight in armour mounted on a horse was the inevitable leader. The development of a military command nexus between landowner and peasant under feudalism, however this originated, has greatly influenced the evolution of the rank structure in Western armies almost up to the present time.

Until well on into our own century the concept of a class of gentry who furnished the officers and of lower orders who furnished the rank and file was widely accepted. In the eighteenth century education was largely confined to the upper classes, where you would also expect to find almost a monopoly of managerial capability, with a confident practice of command based upon the administration of property. The division between those who had been conditioned to exercise command and those who had not was accepted as natural and rational. It was sometimes even argued that heredity had endowed the well-born with a capability to acquire the art of military command which was denied to those of lowlier origin. This, however, was possibly no more than a not very successful attempt to dignify, as a result of the operation of a natural law, what was in fact no more than a product of circumstance.

As war has become more technically complex, class structure in the parent society less rigid and education more widely spread, so has professionalism in military command become more meaningful, more necessary and more widely sought. The method of selection of officers and the criteria of their advancement are very different in the British Army of today from what they were before the First World War.

One method of choosing officers which, on superficial examination, might seem to be particularly acceptable in democratic societies has in recent times proved signally unsuccessful. I refer to the system of election by the rank and file. In three national revolutions, the American, the French and the Russian, the election of officers was introduced quite early on and in all three it was soon discarded.

There are at least two good reasons for this. One is that the qualities likely to appeal to the men in the potential officer were not always those best calculated to make of him an appropriate professional instrument for the carrying out of instructions from above. Armed forces, I have suggested, require a high degree of continuous confidence from top to bottom. The election of officers by those immediately below them has been very far indeed from contributing to this. Another reason is that an elected officer must be gravely hampered in the exercise of authority over those who put him where he is by the knowledge that they can, perhaps, equally readily remove him.

The exercise of military authority in an alliance raises questions of its own. Whom or what does the national officer serve?

The critical point can be found at the level of command where a national contingent in an allied force comes under the command of an officer of some other nation. Below this point the normal procedure to be found within the national hierarchy will tend to be followed without question. The officer placed at this point, however, may find himself in difficulties. He has been commissioned into the service of one country and given a position of authority in it over fellow nationals. He will either have taken a specific oath of allegiance to this country or have been made aware in other ways that it expects his undeviating support. Suppose that his government then decides to place a force, of which he is the commander, at the disposal of an alliance and he finds himself under the orders of an allied commander of some other nationality. What does he do when what he considers to be a conflict arises between what is best for the alliance and what is best for his own country?

It is to be hoped that he will be able to put the interest of the alliance first. For it must be assumed that his own country would not be a party to an alliance if the relevant national objectives could be more readily attained outside it. Subordination of the national interest to that of the alliance must therefore be accepted by the military officer as unavoidable. It is hoped that he will recognise this.

Unfortunately the issues, when a conflict of this sort emerges, are rarely simple or clearly defined. They are more often complex and obscure. The position of an officer holding two positions in an alliance – when he commands a national force, for instance, at the same time as he commands other national components in an international formation – can be particularly difficult. This is less because of the difficulty of making a choice between conflicting obligations (always assuming that philosophically speaking a conflict of duties is possible) than because of the difficulty of determining exactly what the issues are.

In the Northern Army Group of N.A.T.O., for example, the system in fact works smoothly, because staff officers of allied nations (including Britain) are reminded that they must ignore their nationality in handling military problems and never imagine at any level that a sending State posting an officer into a N.A.T.O. appointment can be allowed to regard him, within that appointment, as a national agent.

Nevertheless, in these international complexes cruel problems can arise. A German officer in a N.A.T.O. headquarters, for example, was employed on the targeting of nuclear weapons. Like many other sensitive people he found the thought of nuclear warfare repugnant though he fully accepted the requirement to plan for it. His target areas, however, fell within parts of his own country which, with their people, he knew well and loved. His work distressed him and the more conscientiously he did it the more painful he found it. Before long it became advisable to secure his removal to other work.

The difficulty I have been discussing will continue to arise as far as we can see into the future. It always emerges quite early on in the consideration of integrated multi-national field forces.

At what level do you try to integrate these? The level at which a national group – section, company, brigade, corps or whatever else it may be – is commanded by someone who is himself subordinate to a superior of another nationality is the level at which the problem emerges. This may be depressed as far down as the section or squad of ten men or so, or raised to the level of a corps or above. It cannot be eliminated by the wave of a wand. At that point in the chain of command at which there is a transference of allegiance from a national military entity to an allied entity problems will arise for a long time to come.

In the study of multi-national forces this is a difficulty far transcending in importance the more obvious problems like those of language. It will continue to be so for as long as the nation State retains its present importance in international affairs.

We have been looking at the possibilities of conflict between national interests and the interests of an alliance. There is another sort of conflict which can emerge in even more painful form and is even more difficult to resolve. It arises when a military officer is obliged by the terms of his service to carry out orders which he finds from an ethical point of view repugnant.

The essential form of this conflict can easily be obscured by other factors. The incident on the Curragh in 1914 before the outbreak of the First World War gives an example. The officers of the Cavalry Brigade preferred resignation (which was permissible in peace) to the possibility of having to use force against Ulstermen choosing to retain a closer link with the Crown than Home Rule in Ireland would permit. In this extraordinary affair the issue of how far a properly constituted authority can oblige its military servants to act against their convictions was raised in sharper form than at any time in England since the mid-seventeenth century. In the whole of the Curragh incident, particularly in the way it was handled by the British Government, politics inevitably played a major part and often a dubious one. There is little doubt, however, that an issue of conscience (and certainly one of consistency) can be seen in it and that many of the officers concerned recognised this.

In Syria and the Lebanon after the fall of France in 1940 another interesting situation arose. The officers of the Troupes Françaises du Levant were generally a highly professional body. Their loyalty to the Republic was considerable. The position taken by their seniors, with a high degree of support from below, was essentially that the duty of the force was the defence of these Mandated Territories, against invasion from any source whatsoever, so long as the properly constituted government in France continued to require it. There is no doubt at all that the wish of the overwhelming majority of Frenchmen in the T.F.L. was to fight the Axis. But the Government of Pétain was generally seen by them as the properly constituted Government of the Republic. The orders of this government were to resist the Allies if they attempted to invade Syria and the Lebanon and these orders the T.F.L. carried out.

Their opposition to our entry was stiff. In my own view it might never have been so stiff if (greatly to the surprise of many of us taking part in this operation at a low level) the Free French had not been brought in on the Allied side. This, of course, at once introduced the characteristics of civil war. What ensued was often savage. After the Armistice I met old friends on the Vichy French side who left me in no doubt that many of them had suffered a severe enough crisis of conscience in the first instance. The subsequent requirement to fight not only their allies but their countrymen as well made this position more painful still. But I can remember none who would say they had been wrong in the first place.

A still more important case is that of the German regular officers who rejected Nazi principles but found themselves serving in a war under a properly constituted and fully recognised government which was determined to pursue them. It is impossible not to sympathise with German officers who did not want a Nazi victory and yet saw themselves bound by their professional duty to fight for it. The greatest credit must go to those who attempted to overthrow Hitler and died as a result. It would be quite wrong, however, to deny credit to many other professional officers who deplored the objectives and methods of the Nazi régime perhaps no less deeply, and who showed themselves in battle no less brave, but who did not regard the overthrow of properly constituted government as consistent with the obligations they had assumed. The more firmly a soldier believes in the subordination of military to civil the less easily will he be persuaded to raise a violent hand against his own government.*

Command decisions in the past have been largely intuitive. The introduction of automatic processes may have reduced but has not entirely eliminated the requirement for intuitive command decisions.

What the computer has done is to permit the solution of problems where the factors are all quantifiable, and to assist in the solving of other problems when they are mainly so. The decision-maker can thus be relieved of the necessity to make decisions by mathematical processes which indicate the most profitable course. He is accordingly released for the work which, in the absence of adequate measurements, can only be done intuitively.

The loose and comprehensive term 'morale' embraces a wide span of factors which have hitherto proved incapable of reliable quantification. Morale in warfare, however, continues to be of the very greatest importance. It is not good enough in war games to disregard the moral factor on both sides because it is not quantifiable on either.†

* Mommsen said of Pompey: 'Er gehörte zu den Menschen, die wohl eines Verbrechens fähig sind, aber keiner Insubordination; im guten wie im schlimmen Sinne war er durch und durch Soldat . . . Es ist oft beobachtet worden, dass der Soldat, auch wenn er den Entschluss gefasst hat seinen Vorgesetzten den Gehorsam zu versagen, dennoch, wenn dieser Gehorsam gefordert wird, unwillkürlich wieder in Reihe und Glied tritt. . . .'
This too is fair comment, but possibly more upon the nature of the military institution in Prussia in Mommsen's time than upon the general position, though it also has relevance to the argument here. I am indebted to my old friend Mr. Karl Leyser of Magdalen College, Oxford, for showing me this.
† General Mike West, whose office wall in Washington when he was Chief of the British Defence Liaison Staff was plastered with newspaper headlines saying things like, 'Kremlin accuses West of total depravity', once asked the white-coated man in charge of the war game how many men ran away on either side. None, was the surprised reply. In that case, said the General, the result was worthless. All battles were decided by the numbers who ran away and by nothing else.

Even when components can be fully quantified it is not always the case in battle that sufficient data will be available at the appropriate time for the writing of a programme. Automatic data processing has proved quite indispensable in the development of systems of weapons control, where the components are few (height, speed, angle and distance for instance) and readily measured. It is becoming increasingly useful in the logistical field. But its application in a very wide area of command decision-making has not yet proved possible. Automatic data processing has tended to restrict the area within which intuitive decision alone remains possible. It is very far indeed from eliminating it.

The advent of the computer does not seem likely to have much effect on the sort of considerations raised in this chapter. What is far more important to ask is what the impact might be of the most significant of all developments in the history of war – the introduction of weapons of mass destruction? If a handful of technicians and perhaps a group of brave individual agents can, at the instance of a government, deal a shattering blow at a national opponent, without recourse to the armed forces hitherto furnished by the military institution, will the arguments raised here be any longer relevant?

The simplest answer is that if the fullest capabilities now available for the destruction of man are used the population of the world is doomed. All civilisation of any sort will perish and its institutions will go with it, the military amongst them.

Instruments of mass destruction, however, have been available now for quite a long time. Bacteriological warfare has long been possible. Chemical warfare was tried in World War I but did not appear in World War II to any important extent, even though its techniques had in the meantime been improved. We have now lived with the possibilities of nuclear war for a quarter of a century – not a long time, it is true, but still not insignificant. It seems just possible that we may learn to live indefinitely with the means of mass destruction and not employ them. Proliferation presents a problem. But man is a clever little monkey – much too clever, in fact, and not nearly good enough – and will survive on this earth if he can. My own possibly rather optimistic view is that he will.

The existence of weapons of mass destruction will make an unrestricted war suicidal. This is unlikely to prevent the application of force. Military operations of lesser scope than general war would therefore appear unavoidable. The military institution collapses when the man in the white coat takes over. But so does everything else. Until then the military will remain an essential feature of human society.

I write near the end of a professional military career after some thirty-five years spent as a regular soldier. If I had known before it began what I know now I believe my choice would still have been the same. I have yet to meet a man who has made his career in any of the Services, whatever rank he may have reached in it, who says anything different. My own time as a professional soldier has taken me from a university, through a world war, into active service both before this war and after it, from fighting as a horse soldier through fighting in tanks and as a parachutist, along normal lines of employment on the staff and in command to a post as Commander-in-Chief. What I have had to say in this chapter about authority in military service in general is the result of reflection during my own. I now wish in this concluding section to bring together the main points of the argument as I see it, with a few further comments.

There is no sign whatever that man will soon desist from the application of physical force to the solution of social problems. Force still remains the ultimate sanction in human affairs and this is likely to be so as far as we can see. Armed forces are therefore of high importance to sovereign States for without them sovereignty can only be exercised in diminished degree.

The military institution is the formal framework within which the State is furnished with the armed forces it requires. Those who serve as professionals in these forces follow the profession of arms, whose business is the ordered application of force at the instance of properly constituted authority. The life these men lead is the military life.

This does not make of the man who follows it a militarist. Armed forces, in our own country at any rate, contain few militarists. Nor does it cause him to cease to be a citizen. It does, however, set him apart from other citizens.

The military institution may be important in contemporary society in the same sort of way as military force: more, that is, by virtue of what it is than what it does. To dismantle it, or to reduce it to insignificance, would not only deprive government of an instrument for the projection of external policies. It would also deprive the parent society of a component demonstrating the virtues (and, if you like, the disadvantages or even the vices as well) of an ordered way of life.

A distinguishing feature of the military institution is its dependence upon a framework of authority. Those who embrace the profession of arms and enter the military life must accept this. They must expect to find themselves, so long as they serve, both under authority to other men and having other men set in authority under them. They accept, as servicemen, in our own country at any rate, the ultimate supreme authority of the State. They do this without question.

Since the conduct of battle is the basic function of armed forces, and this demands authoritative direction, armed forces can scarcely be organised in any other way than in an authoritative and hierarchic structure. Authority is in the military institution the essence of the whole.

Military authority, therefore, is indispensable in our society, for without it government would be unable to apply one of its essential instruments.

But military authority is not only indispensable, it is probably in itself more good than bad. It is also a producer of good.

As the essential condition without which the military institution cannot exist military authority can be held in large part responsible for the development of the virtues which the military institution requires. These include fortitude, unselfishness, loyalty and integrity. These are qualities desirable in any group of men. In the military group they are functionally indispensable.

The presence of a repository of these virtues in our society cannot be without advantages. The existence of an institution which encourages them and at the same time demands an ordered way of life brings benefits to that society beyond those offered to the State by the successful discharge of the institution's primary function. It sets an example and establishes desirable standards of conduct. The only question that can reasonably arise here is whether these benefits are too dearly bought. I have yet to hear this rationally debated.

Military authority is not only good: it is also a producer of good. Those who live an ordered life usually find that it is a good life. To be one of those set in authority with men under command is a liberating experience.

The acceptance of the role seems on the whole likely to make better people. Like those who practise Christianity (as most serving officers do) military men may not all be very good. Most, however, are probably a great deal better than they would otherwise have been.

The military man will be likely to respect order and to reject disorder. It may seem to him that what contributes to order serves powers of light, what contributes to disorder serves powers of darkness. In many military men there is more than a trace of the Manichee.

He is required by his contract to accept risk to his own life and to be prepared to take the lives of others. I do not think I ever met a professional soldier who had become one because he wanted to kill. Whatever may have been the case in times long gone by, a man who joined the British Army today for this reason would be someone the Company Commander would get rid of at the earliest possible moment after he had found out why the man was there. Nevertheless a soldier's weapons are designed for maximum lethality and destructiveness combined with maximum economy. He is taught to apply them with maximum efficiency. His weapon training concerns itself much more with questions of precision, speed, safety, response and control than with effects. His tactical and other training (logistical, for example) concerns itself with the application, support and direction of the whole on clearly aggressive lines. There is little doubt that military training leads off aggressive tendencies and this is probably one reason why the military man, in spite of the nature of his calling, is so often in himself compassionate and humane. He also on the whole tends to have a respect for truth, generosity and humility. He is more likely than not to be repelled by falsehood, meanness and spiritual pride. Sublimation may be at work here too. So also is the orderliness of a life regulated by authority towards a functional end in which valuable moral qualities are indispensable.

The good soldier does not often meet the standards of Wordsworth's 'Happy Warrior' – 'that every man at arms would wish to be'. But he is rarely Schweik – or Wozzeck – who illuminate, of course, the human condition in general far more than any specifically military aspect of it.

War may be degrading. The preparation of men for it is almost certainly not. In judging the military it must be remembered that it is easy to point to the worst products of any process but misleading to claim that they are typical. It is even more misleading to claim that they are without exception the only products. In judging any way of life it is sensible not to look at its worst respresentatives, and reflect how bad they are, but to look upon the best it has produced and judge its value upon its capability for producing these.*

Man, so like an angel, still obstinately remains a good deal less. His apparent imperfectability is a source of sadness, disappointment and frustration to very many. Some find this situation so vexing that they are inclined to lose patience with the very existence of agencies which would not, of course, be needed if man were perfect. Armed forces figure prominently here. So do police. Men animated by the very highest aspirations are often less than charitable about those whose presence among them is clear evidence that man still has a long way to go.

The availability of weapons of mass destruction does not remove the requirement for military authority as we have come to know it. Forms of warfare less than total war now become not less likely than they were but more. Armed forces will be required as far into the future as we can see. The pattern of mili-

---

* A reviewer of books, who had been a regular soldier, and on his own confession a failure at it, said in a weekly a year or two ago (if I remember rightly) that regular Army officers are without exception drunken, idle and feckless. I cannot help thinking that this is about as sensible as saying that reviewers of books are without exception temperate, industrious and provident.

tary authority under which they operate will persist. The ordered life of the professional man at arms, lived within that framework, will continue to be a feature of our society. I cannot believe that this will be the poorer or the worse for that.

Chairman, Women's Royal Voluntary Service

To link authority to the field of philanthropy and voluntary organisations is, in my opinion, really to offer those who are working in this realm of personal service a means of guidance and safeguarding. I suppose I say this because my experience has been at a time when charitable patronage of past years has given way to statutory aid of today and, in their best form, statutory bodies could and should be the ideal authority for guiding, aiding, supporting and, if necessary, in certain circumstances, adjusting the work of voluntary organisations.

As one examines the various forms of voluntary work one realises that the object is a need for alleviation of suffering and an aim to be set. The mere fact that a great deal of voluntary participation in any form of work stems from the worker being animated by a feeling of sentiment in regard to the person to be helped can very often be the seed of danger to the worker. The Charity Commissioners, a safeguard of infinite value and authority, came into existence in 1853 and from decade to decade have been strengthened in order to be able, by means of the authority vested in them, to protect those who are wanting to practise true philanthropy, in the best sense of the word, from the sharks who could and sometimes do destroy them.

Voluntary service before the war was in most countries dominated by charitable patronage. The accumulating of cash for the carrying through of a specific voluntary undertaking very often gave a pre-emption to those of personal position and very often gave a pre-emption to those of personal position or possession and the collecting of large sums of money often appeared to be the be-all and end-all of a charitable undertaking. There is no longer any question but that voluntary service,

174

Voluntary Organisations and Philanthropy

instead of being a development of charitable patronage, is today an integration of the gift, by an individual, of his time, his skill and his energy into the statutory aid of the land. This has resulted in broadening the basis on which the nation has the participation of many more persons in its day-to-day living and, in this way, more has been learned about the community by such participants and there is more recognition by them of the needs of the community. The very nature of voluntary service and its infinite permutations indicate an especial need for the support of authority, although the mere whisper of dictation from authority would upset many worthwhile undertakings!

All true philanthropy must be built on a faith or philosophy and an examination of how this 'building' should be pursued inevitably shows the need for certain basic principles to be laid down. Legal rules which safeguard the undertaking itself must be observed; rigid financial obligations to prevent miscarriage of aim must be accepted; and, above all, and ever-present in any work of this type, safeguards against the misuse of cash must be studied. In relation to voluntary organisations and philanthropy in the broadest possible sense authority has been established by such rules, regulations and, indeed, laws, and these, which constitute a safe foundation on which to build, are welcomed by a *bona-fide* worker and invoked as a strength of immense value on countless occasions by every philanthropic body. But, in this type of work, authority is best accepted when seen and used as a support and not as a despotic control, because the very nature of the commodity under discussion needs such careful handling that it would dry up were it to think that local authorities, central government or any persons classed as 'them' were dictating a policy which, from the

175

workers' point of view, comes entirely from their own outlook and their own volition.

Today, statutory aid demands definite standards and skills in its accredited professionals and the voluntary workers of today must recognise this and, in addition, fit themselves to be accepted as worthwhile helpers to those who carry the ultimate authority.

Statutory bodies have understandably hesitated to accept voluntary workers on a full-time commitment, but they have been wise in giving voluntary organisations an opportunity to prove themsleves and, where they have found such bodies reliable and good, they have had the courage to sub-contract to them specific jobs, always insisting on safeguards in regard to standards, continuity and control of finance.

The acquiring of confidence by the public in the volunteer depends so largely on the standard of work done by that volunteer that it is absolutely necessary to translate to the volunteers that their work must be of an even better calibre than work done for material gain. This is because, in all things, the unknown person doing the job has to be much better than the known one if he is to gain the confidence of the general public or of the people he is serving. This acquiring of confidence through work done has a much greater value and a much broader implication than just the carrying through of a specific job, for it is ultimately responsible for the confidence accorded to the members of the team as well as to voluntary services generally.

What is the ultimate contribution of voluntary service to the nation? I believe it can supply an element of moral strength by the participation of the individual in creating a national conscience which, ultimately, cannot but be of value to the country.

Philanthropy and, indeed, voluntary service (which for this purpose should be quoted as one) does, because the word 'philanthropy' means the love of humans, stem from a concept in the individual's mind, from a readiness to give in the person's mentality, and from the stimulus brought to bear on those who have neither thought nor felt, by those who have done so, in order to activate them into a way of thinking. The objective, in its various forms, is always the same, the fact that certain people recognise the need, that that recognition is strengthened by either experience or information or personal knowledge, and, therefore, that the wish, the urge, the zest to help can be passed on to others, so that, in fact, the task can be accomplished and the aim can be met.

In the first place, the person who is to be in charge does have to think very deeply in relation to using the fund of readiness to serve that is available and this is where authority is of infinite value. In a village the natural tendency is for one person to help the other especially when in trouble; but the nasty old man, the dirty old woman, the unacceptable family, go by the board and although, in the past, charitable patronage has looked after most of those who needed care, nevertheless it is indisputable that statutory aid made available by law is required for those who fall by the wayside and do not come within the understanding and compassion of human sentiment.

What a nation really requires from voluntary service is a contribution, within the community, by thinking and responsible citizens, for the good of that community. This contribution must be given in the shape in which it is *needed*, and must set a true example, so that others, seeing it, will have confidence in such service and wish to contribute themselves.

Through experiment, and especially because of its variety, voluntary service can undoubtedly demonstrate the willingness of responsible people to serve the needs of the community and to show something of the urge and the readiness there is in the community to meet them. This must not be underestimated as to its difficulty but at the same time can undoubtedly be accepted as something of real worth from the point of view of a contribution to the unseen strength and character of the nation.

In this country the most useful person, who gives what is recognised as a national service, came into being through the philanthropic work of voluntary organisation. I mean the district nurse who, if a true census were possible, would to my mind be found to be the most popular person *per se* in the whole of Great Britain. This popularity is built entirely on the person-

M

ality of the type of woman who is doing the work, on the way she spends herself and is therefore truly a 'friend of human beings' and also on the fact that her service is of such infinite value in its simple form of ready help in time of need that everyone trusts her. But authority is there to back her and is, of course, a very great strength.

To trace this example from start to finish one must accept that originally the idea was conceived, the scheme was thought out and tested, and subsequently the funds were raised, in a variety of ways by a series of local efforts of a philanthropic nature but nevertheless of a charitable make-up district nurses as we know them were set up. Through the passage of time they became more and more established until, with the advent of the Welfare State, they have been absorbed into the whole and are today part of the local authority service, and, in their final shape, they have brought with them the tradition of strength, the personality of the worker, and have remained of inestimable value to the country. They have behind them the authority of their own training, of their Association and of local government and, as such, both the public and the worker are guaranteed in the continuity of their service by authority as it has developed.

Voluntary service in its ultimate and best form is a way of thinking and a way of living. It takes endless thinking to create and it takes endless work to evolve and those who are the motivators of others have to recognise from the start that without:

(a) recognised authority,

(b) the right to invoke the rules of authority as and when needed, and

(c) the overhauling and seeing that authority fits the need, their own work would suffer greatly. This has been proved over and over again and if one were to compare pre-war and post-war 'authority' in this field one could judge relative responsibilities, values and the recognition of those hazards which have led to the creation of excellent safeguards.

In the field of voluntary service whose main 'output' is philanthropic and therefore whose persons-in-charge have as a main task the co-ordinating, canalising, channeling, and safeguarding of finance, a matter of paramount importance is to be sure of how to achieve the objective with the maximum results and the minimum hazards. This is where the real understanding of the true use of authority comes in. It is no longer a question of the steel hand in the velvet glove – it is much more like the nylon thread within the foam rubber coating. So many people seem to forget that they are handling other people's money and that it is more important to be meticulous about other people's cash than it is when handling one's own and, because of this fact, and because it is necessary to watch and to guard finance down to the last penny, rules and regulations which often seem restricting to the unthinking public must exist in relation to any single undertaking which either collects or spends or handles in any way the cash donated by other people. The law of the land is today such that if one appeals for a certain aim and the Trust registered for that aim has the holding of the money, it is the ultimate responsibility of the people in charge to see that that undertaking is fully honoured. The ultimate authority at a series of different levels is vested in the Charity Commissioners and, although the support and control of authority are felt as a steel hand within the proverbial velvet glove, nevertheless they are, in fact, of extreme value to the many endeavours they serve. This, I contend, is because through a rigid interpretation of the integrity necessary in handling other people's money the application itself gets translated into every sphere of work and builds a strong make-up in those who are practising the principles.

It would be foolish to ignore the fact that in the particular field under consideration there is a very great chance for misuse of funds and that those who are in Ultimate Authority (with a capital 'U' and a capital 'A') are in fact responsible for watching those who would like to make 'a quick return for cash'. It is for this reason that we have authority controlling this that and the other, and it is for this reason that we have authority controlling flag days, controlling trust funds, and it is for this reason that those who are responsible for individual undertakings recognise how foolish they would be if they did not avail themselves to the utmost of the help that such authority can provide.

To use authority in the right way, I believe it is necessary to think philosophically, to examine deeply and to establish fundamentally the principles on which, whatever the work may be, it should be undertaken. The outlook of the individual will in the aggregate influence the outlook of the many. This is why it is necessary in the first place to evolve the machinery for any undertaking so that the weakness of the individual can be safe-guarded and the strength of the individual can be exploited. This, basically, means that if a concept is a clear and good one and if it can be shown to others in a simple enough shape, with easy enough machinery and a minimum number of rules and regulations, it can then be translated to layer after layer of people without distortion, with a maximum amount of under-standing and a minimum amount of misunderstanding. This is one of the most important cardinal principles in the organising of voluntary service.

The first necessity of any voluntary enterprise and, indeed, of any philanthropic aim is to discover not only the need, but what is being done by other people to meet that need, so as to ascertain that there will be no overlapping and to be certain that the need is a real one and not a fictitious idea that has sprung up in the brain of somebody who wishes to do something! This may sound rather hard-boiled but it is necessary, because the safeguarding of other people's energies, time and ability is just as important in its own way as the safeguarding of cash. Today, with the Welfare State and statutory responsibility at local authority level, it is much easier to check in this particular way than it was in days gone by. The registration of charities undertaken centrally but now listed at local level has simplified many things. The fact that one can, by merely calling at the responsible office and checking, find out what is deemed to be done is the first step towards finding out whether in fact it is being done and, if not, consequently and subsequently going ahead with the job itself.

Many accusations of inefficiency and lack of method have been levelled at voluntary bodies. I remember the first time I used a dictaphone. I was asked to say who should give a certain lecture somewhere and how that lecture should be defined as well as what particular subject it should deal with.

In dictating into the dictaphone I said, 'Please ask Miss So-and-so: the name of her talk should be, "W.V.S., a Voluntary Service and the Sources of Supplies it brings with it".' Fortunately, in evolving the machinery of our own Service, we had made it quite clear that nothing should ever go out to anybody in the way of the written word unless it had been signed or initialled by the person who had dictated it and, even more important, that it should always have been read by the person from whom it emanated. My shock was great when the note came to me for initialling and read, 'Ask Miss So-and-so, and call her talk, "W.V.S., a Volatile Service, and the Series of Surprises it brings with it"!'.

I can only think that the girl who typed the tape knew a good deal about a great many philanthropic enterprises and had a poor opinion of them, and that this was undoubtedly based on the local level of a number of bodies that had come into existence rather haphazardly and had failed to prove themselves to be what a good and worthwhile undertaking should be.

The question of cash has been discussed often, safeguards in this direction are many, and the Charity Commission has not only a very responsible position in regard to cash and kind, but in addition has a very real understanding of its subject. The Charity Commission itself knows the hazards of over-specialisation and over-itemising. There is no question at all that many people feel the tragedy, for instance, of money which was from a specialised point of view set up hundreds of years ago 'to provide red flannel petticoats for old ladies whose names were Tabitha' and now naturally has no outlet.

The public are generous beyond words and the call on the public is still, to my mind, too easily permitted because those who can ill-afford to do so are moved by the nature of the appeal and deprive themselves to contribute their half-crown, but the total contributed often amounts to a huge sum and is used with less forethought than is worthy of the sacrifice that the individual has made.

The Charity Commission of Great Britain is such that other countries envy it. In all things in this regard they should be looked to as the ultimate authority, with rules and regulations as to the local application and proving that the law of the land exists as the over-all umbrella authority.

There are many rules, some of which may be regarded as tedious: but experience shows them to be good. They have to do either with cash (which often involves vast amounts and large figures) or kind, which involves bricks and mortar and all sorts and kinds of possessions.

I believe that philanthropy started with the religious bodies many centuries ago and from them have come not only the hospital services and welfare services of the country but subsequently the education and the law of the land. In turn this philanthropy has gone through many changes, and at the time when men and women invested any funds they had in buying large acreages, the tenants on that land in turn 'tamed' the owners and taught them of the demands and needs of human beings and called forth their compassion. Since the time that men and women have spent their large sums of money on racing motor cars, diamonds and aeroplanes, this taming of the individual has not come to pass in the same way and therefore another method of generating his contribution (beyond the casual signing of a cheque) is necessary.

It is for this reason that the volunteer is today of such tremendous importance. If, in fact, volunteers are of great worth they must be given a fair opportunity and a full understanding of what they are undertaking and why they are doing so. This is necessary because other people's endeavours are the make-up of voluntary service. The individual is the key to all things in this field. The shape of the contribution that the individual gives must be of a type that can in turn be useful and merged into the whole.

If this premise is acceptable and if the volunteer is looked upon as a person of real worth it is because of his contribution. This contribution must be his own outlook, and if he is prepared to give generously, not merely of what he can do but of what he is, then it is very necessary to recognise that the contribution is a very special one and, indeed, one that could not be bought for any amount of money because the purchase of that commodity would injure the commodity itself. I believe that the contribution of a really worthwhile volunteer is beyond price and must be valued and handled as such. A person who is a convinced volunteer will do things nobody else in the world would do and therefore there is a very great responsibility on whoever is handling that volunteer.

One of the drawbacks in arguing this point is that there is no variable by which one can measure those things that are done by volunteers. They are not able to be touched by the hand or weighed in scales and yet, sometimes, I wonder whether it is not a good thing that the standard does not exist and that the analysis has not been undertaken, so that things that are of infinite worth may not be handled roughly by unthinking people and hurt in the handling. Nobody can tell what has gone into the make-up of the undertaking of an individual. Nobody can tell, for sure, what first activated an individual towards spending himself for others. Nobody can evaluate how it is that an individual, glimpsing the pain that others suffer, the generosity with which others give or the ability that others have, does in fact undertake himself and prove by devotion that the contribution of the volunteer is far beyond anything that could be attained in the commercial market.

Some people would think that the person handling the volunteer represents authority to the volunteer himself. I believe this is wrong. I believe that if too formal a hierarchy of authority is established it can create a feeling which is not good for the aim of the service itself. Therefore I should like to advocate that authority, and I would insist on the word 'authority', in any shape is support and that the person within the hierarchy who carries the responsibility is in support of the person with the seemingly less important job, but perhaps the much more worthwhile job, inasmuch as it is touching and influencing a human being's whole life. If this be accepted, then support instead of command becomes of real worth and support has the additional value of demanding humility from the giver of it and very often of stopping any ambition towards climbing to great heights for personal motives.

Many years ago in serious conversation with Eleanor Roosevelt, a very great woman, I asked what she thought was the finest attribute of any person she had ever met. Without pondering (as she usually did) on the question she answered:

'There is no question at all, humility, and in my long life I have seen it only twice, in its full perfection, and both times the people were near saints!' This is tragically true, and this therefore has to be the authority which governs the discipline and the thinking of whoever is in charge of other volunteers. This is not a Uriah Heep attitude or anything of the sort – it is a question of constant revision of self and constant pruning of one's own habits and methods of living, administering or organising in order to get rid of those things which are not in the nature of humility, and in learning those things which would be more easily accepted by the volunteers working with one.

Too many things have been done too often by people in order to try to climb the ladder of self-advancement. This has very often happened within philanthropic and voluntary service itself. It is to be hoped that in the years ahead a purging of this side of endeavour may be achieved and that purity of motive in understanding the undertaking and the seriousness of the responsibility may temper action, so that the work as a whole comes more into line with the faith or philosophy which has generated the undertaking in the first place.

I believe that the absence of a binding contract in the way of either cash received or document signed does, with many people, because there is no material gain, become a contribution so dedicated that, instead of having a material tie, there is a spiritual one that is, in fact, much stronger. There follows that there is no necessity to accept that one faith, one outlook or one professed religion holds a pre-emption over another. It is a question of belief and personal character and in this matter religion and beliefs can be as varied as can be personalities.

Experience of many years has taught me that no regimentation meted out to the volunteer is really of worth and the more comfortable the background supplied to the volunteer the less the stimulus it provides to the individual to carry out the job. One learns that if volunteers are to be able they must be happy and if they are happy it must be arranged so that they bring their own initiative into the work and use their own techniques and their own methods.

There is the real need to have varied and responsible support for those doing the work at every level; an awareness of responsibility and confidence that other people will not fear that they will be let down because discipline is sufficient to hold oneself in control and to be able to do those things which are needed of one. This is the authority of self-generated control which is necessary to win the trust of the volunteer.

I speak naturally as one who has worked with women for many years. With a woman one can tell her what is needed and where it is needed and why and one can have a thousand per cent co-operation; but one must not tell her how to do the job. One can give her hints and advice but if one tells her how to do the job one is merely wasting time and encouraging disruption because no woman will do a practical job in the way that another woman suggests! What one has to do is to make her realise that what matters is the job and not the person doing the job and that it is necessary for the person undertaking it to get the task carried through however difficult it is.

Fundamentally, there is no sense in thinking that certain people are the types to make good volunteers and that they should be of a pattern. The more variety there is the better the performance and the better lesson it is to the person in support. Volunteers do not just give of their leisure; many of them – the vast majority – have to make their leisure to give it and, as with the tithes of old, so can it be argued that the person who just gives the tithe without effort is doing so from habit and not from conviction.

Today the young are idealistic beyond belief – they would serve in any way which appeals to their hopes and they give really generously. They are intelligent, clever and open-handed and because of their thoughtful outlook I am sure they will always welcome authority in this field for the reason that they can see its value and can make use of its support.

There is an obligation, I believe, to realise that the character of this country has been recognised throughout the world by the acceptance of the fact that 'an Englishman's word is as good as his bond' and each one of us must support the belief that once a job has been accepted that job is a binding factor. What, in the final count, is the cash with which one is paid? It is no more than an instrument for bartering. And what is the payment for voluntary service? – human relationship, the accomplishment of an aim and the achievement of an undertaking. If the scales of judgment were available to balance them it is to be wondered which of the two would have more weight.

In many countries, and indeed internationally, philanthropy has occasionally had a bad name both because of the unreliability of the people handling the undertaking, and because voluntary service has been deemed to be unreliable due to the lack of continuity it has sometimes shown. Both these things are unforgiveable. If a man's word is as good as his bond, so should his undertaking be, whether in the field of philanthropic endeavour or in the area of voluntary participation, and he should serve just in the same way as if he were in receipt of a salary. The fact that the final forfeit for one would be loss of cash is balanced by the fact that the forfeit for the other would be loss of confidence and if the citizens of Great Britain do not value the second much higher than the first a mighty effort is required to re-establish the viewpoint which has built our nation.

I believe profoundly that the ultimate strength of a nation lies in her character and not just in her commercial achievement; I believe that the ultimate wealth of a nation is not found in her financial genius but in the character of her people, and I hold that as that ultimate strength lies in every thinking man and woman who make up the nation, so it is necessary for each man and woman to know of principles far outside their day to day living and to practise their beliefs to the full.

Sir Stanley Rous, C.B.E., J.P.

President, Federation Internationale
de Football Association
Chairman of the Executive Committee of
the Central Council for Physical Recreation

Because young people all over the world tend to be more vociferous than they were, and in many respects more herdlike, the impression is given that 'mere anarchy is let loose upon the world . . . and innocence is drowned'. Perhaps the young *are* more violent and, if so, it cannot be all their own fault: it should be remembered that they have been raised in times of violence and unrest.

It could also be said that we have all been members of a younger generation: what could be more shattering to a young man than to be hauled away from his career to serve his country in a six-year war? Certainly the Second World War affected the lives and careers of thousands and thousands of promising sportsmen. The late forties saw the twilight performances of cricketers and footballers, athletes and lawn tennis players (so far as first-class, organised sport was concerned) which, in a sense, were strange to see, for what would have been their peak years in such competition had so much time not been passed in graver occupations?

The actions and opinions of the young attract so much attention these days because they represent a whole new class of society – the teenagers. Not so long ago – or so it seems to me – a boy or a girl knew only that as time went by he or she would, by the nature of things, 'grow up'. In my day there was nothing to worry about in being a minor; in fact one always felt sorry for the adults who seemed to have so many burdens and anxieties peculiar to their status in society. Time enough, one

Sport

felt, for adulthood, fatherhood, rates and taxes, the responsibility of putting in a Member of Parliament and so on. As youngsters we had our own world to deal with: there were lessons to be learned, schoolmasters to be placated, friends to be made and, alas, to be lost.

Most important of all to an active boy, there was sport to be played and enjoyed. And in this field there was no resentment, as I remember it, against authority. The games master – poor fellow – had the job of organising our football, our cricket, our swimming, our annual sports. I think we knew that if it had been left to us we should have enjoyed ourselves much less and, if we were really serious about one sport or another, there would have been no great maturing of our skills. But for the master, who would have settled our impassioned disputes over offside – or whether Jones Minor was in fact l.b.w.? All boys are unruly if they have any spirit at all, but they also recognise that without some form of authority and leadership this unruliness, healthy enough in moderation, can degenerate into sheer mob rule.

There are good leaders and bad leaders; loyal and intelligent followers and blind and treacherous followers. Who, as a boy, did not feel sick at heart to witness – or, worse still, become involved with – a small gang of boys led by a notorious bully? A conference would be held, a victim selected – usually a boy who qualified in their parlance as a 'freak', meaning that he had poor eyesight and blinked behind spectacles, or suffered from acne and was awkward because of it – and then the 'gang' would lie in wait and, at a given signal, pounce. It is the pattern for mob riots throughout history: a mass of weak and misguided people led by a lout who thinks himself no end of a fellow because of the number of his followers. If opposition is

189

organised and their activities are challenged, the followers tend to vanish with the utmost rapidity and the bully may find himself in just such a situation as did Benito Mussolini – once cheered and lauded, then reviled and executed.

I was a schoolmaster myself for fourteen years, and what I had learned as a boy among boys was extremely useful to me when I found myself in charge of them. I knew that boys despise weakness and indecision but that 'strong-arm' tactics, though effective, prevent a master from experiencing that most rewarding of all human experience, a genuine and warm-hearted relationship with his pupils. Just as a master has a right to expect a boy to earn whatever recognition can be gained from his work or play, so a master, too, has to earn that boy's reciprocal respect. This can happen only if the master is scrupulously fair, strict but not to the point of being a dictator, and patient with the gropings of a mind that welcomes fresh knowledge but must feel it is necessary, useful knowledge, not something that has to be crammed into him for the sake of cramming.

With the Football Association and F.I.F.A., and as chairman of the executive committee of the Central Council of Physical Recreation, I have had much to do with the teaching and encouragement of sport. And it has always seemed to me that it is as important to teach a young man how to behave as a sportsman as to teach him the technique and strategy of a game.

Harry Altham, founder-president of the English Schools' Cricket Association and an M.C.C. president not long before he died, put it this way in relation to cricket: 'Cricket is, in a sense, warfare in miniature, and a cricket match should be fought out by both sides with all the resources of spirit and technique at their command. At the same time it should always be a recreation, a game to be played not only according to written laws but in harmony with an unwritten code of chivalry and good temper. A cricket team should feel that they are playing with, as well as against, their opponents.'

The ideal of fair play is closely associated with the British race, and long may it be so. We should be hypocrites if we were to claim that in all our dealings with other races, other nations we have remained absolutely faithful to that creed.

There are chapters in our history, as in the histories of other great nations, that cannot be read or remembered without a sense of shame. But man is far from perfect; and at least we can admit to *feeling* shame when considering certain episodes of sheer opportunism and, perhaps, brutality.

I have always believed that sport is the clearest and most positive channel through which the young may appreciate exactly why authority, wisely administered, is so essential to life.

It is impossible to enjoy playing or watching a game when the laws or rules of that game are being disregarded or flouted. And then there is Harry Altham's wonderful phrase about playing a game 'not only according to written, but in harmony with an unwritten code of chivalry and good temper'. I have often heard it said that a game should be played for its own sake and not for its results. For instance, in the pavilion after any club cricket match you will hear someone say, 'I don't play to win. What does it matter if you win or lose? Play the game for its own sake, that's what I say.'

Most of us would agree with this point of view if its specific meaning was that after doing one's utmost to achieve a result on the field of play, one did not crow over a win or weep over a defeat. But all too often it simply means that a person is incapable of playing a game wholeheartedly, to the absolute limit of his capabilities, and after it is all over and perhaps he or his side has lost, of having the philosophic mind and grace of manner to acknowledge that, at least on that day, he has been bettered.

The only reason that a result has any importance is that it is a true measure of skill. The purpose of framing a set of laws for any game and having them administered by a referee or an umpire on the field of play, and for that official's decisions, if fairly arrived at, to be upheld by a legislative association which can make ultimate decisions for the whole sport, is to ensure that competition is indeed fair and just, and that, so far as is humanly possible, conditions are the same for one contestant as for another.

The Football Association, which I served for a great part of my life, is such a body in respect of all organised football – junior or senior, amateur or professional – played in England.

Similar associations operate in Wales, Scotland and Northern Ireland, and, of course, in almost every country in the world. In 1904 the Federation of International Football Associations, of which I am proud to be president, was formed as the organiser and arbiter in the larger realm.

In this one sport, then, a sport which has every claim to be the most widely played throughout the world, authority has been recognised by generation after generation of players, officials, clubs and spectators. It has never been imposed authority; just as the smallest football club in the land elects its own chairman, its secretary, its treasurer, its captains and vice-captains, so those who have served the game administratively have been elected to their positions after proving their quality of leadership to the various strata of football.

Naturally there are always the few who resent any kind of authority and try to make their own laws. We have all seen the kind of footballer who hopes to twist the game his own way by unfair means – by kicking, pushing, tripping or even punching an opponent on the blind side of the referee; and the other kind who tries delaying tactics when a free-kick or throw-in is awarded to his opponents. There is also the player who pretends to be more sinned against than sinning and throws his hands high into the air at every decision, with the idea of getting the referee so harassed that he will lose control of the game and thus play into the hands of the lawless ones.

Sometimes it must seem that far more of this kind of behaviour goes on in first-class professional football than in other levels of competition. But one should always bear in mind that so great is the press, radio and television concentration upon League and Cup matches that the smallest incident before sixty or seventy thousand spectators can assume giant proportions.

Allowing for this, is the referee's authority flouted more frequently and more drastically nowadays than ever before? Reluctantly one must admit that the 'I'm all right, Jack' attitude which became so noticeable immediately after the Second World War *has* produced situations for which it is difficult to find a parallel in pre-war years.

Players and officials walking off the field after a match have been injured by stones, bottles and other missiles thrown at them by vicious louts. This has happened in more than one country and in varying degrees of seriousness. There have also been riots among spectators, with the whole rows of seats burned or hurled on to the ball park; and club offices have been wrecked.

In this respect sport has suffered from the prevailing winds of change – the unpleasant as well as the inspiring ones. The dropping of the first nuclear bomb on Hiroshima should have been the signal to us that never again could we turn to war as the alternative to trying to live together in peace, no matter what colour our skins are or what language we speak. This knowledge imposes an inner discipline on mankind the strain of which erupts in riots, rebellions, so-called 'conventional' war and civil upsets of every kind.

Could this not be at least part of the reason why every country has its roving hooligans, its bottle-throwers, its tele-phone-kiosk wreckers, its assassins or would-be assassins of men in high public office? The obvious and perhaps the only way ahead for mankind is towards a world state, a world parliament, a world police force; a step in this direction was taken by the establishment of the United Nations. Men of goodwill every-where are working unremittingly to bring about the integration of peoples, which does not imply that every nation has to adopt a uniform ideology; merely that every nation should acknow-ledge the right of every human being to freedom of worship, a decent standard of living and, within reasonable limits, freedom of expression.

The mark of a civilised nation is that its leaders think before they talk and talk before they act. Naturally this can lead to a plethora of commissions, working parties, report stages and so on, with a resultant frustration for more forceful characters. But patience *is* rewarded. Far better to endure many a pro-tracted committee session and to feel that at least everyone has had a chance to put his opinion or to state his case, than to settle for one dominant leader who overrides all policies and opinions contrary to his own or, to preserve his status, kills new ideas at birth. There is still a great deal to be said for authority invested in an elected body, the basis of democratic government.

N

How indicative of Britain's attitude to overall authority is the Government's formation of a Sports Council as a 'purely advisory body'. The Sports Council came out of the findings and recommendations of the Wolfenden Committee. But long before the publication of the Wolfenden Report, *Sport and the Community*, the leading sports administrators had been thinking and talking of the much needed national and regional development of sport. One thing was certain: any government that advocated complete state control of sport would have a very rough passage.

Once the Sports Council was formed, with its constituent Regional Sports Councils, its chairman, Mr. Dennis Howell, Minister with a special responsibility for sport, was constantly reminding his listeners in his round-the-country speeches that it was not in his power, nor was it his own or the government's wish, to take the initiative away from local authorities. The function of the Sports Council was to stimulate people to form their own local Sports Advisory Councils which, by means of planning and research, could assess their own needs in the field of sport and recreational facilities. Only at that point would the Sports Council step in, with professional advice on whether it considered a project sound or practicable and, if so, with a recommendation to the appropriate ministry for loan sanction or grant aid if such help were needed.

The co-operation between the Sports Council and the Central Council of Physical Recreation, of whose executive committee I am chairman, has happily been achieved at national as well as at regional level, and this too is indicative of the British instinct towards intelligent partnership rather than stubborn separatism.

It occurs to me at this point that perhaps people are more ready to accept authority in their sporting activities because sport has already undergone its revolution – in the United Kingdom at any rate. Gone are the days when some sports were socially beyond the pale. At one time you could say that cricket and lawn tennis, rugby football and athletics, sailing and ski-ing, squash rackets and badminton were practised mainly by the 'leisured classes'; while association football (long after its confinement to the universities, the common people being expected to devote all their energies to archery) and cycling, weight lifting and wrestling, bowls and coarse fishing were typical interests of the working classes. Golf, too, except in Scotland where it has always been the people's game, was far too costly to be followed by anyone in a humble situation.

Today it is all very different. In spite of economic 'freezes' and wage restraints, our standard of living in the British Isles is both higher and more widely spread. Every weekend you can see whole families going off in their cars to sail or canoe or water-ski; the golf courses are so crowded that golfers have to book days ahead for the chance of a few rounds; and the same is true of the squash courts in private clubs or at sports centres. Lawn tennis courts are to be found in practically every public park in Britain; and although county cricket is slightly on the decline, club cricket is healthy enough and caters for a wider cross-section of the community than ever before.

As for association football, the 'cloth cap' era is very much a thing of the past. First-class clubs have had to modernise their grounds and provide a greater proportion of seats under cover for a spectator public that has become more selective, more sophisticated. The excellent television coverage of the 1966 World Cup matches has attracted more women to league and cup football, and women would never endure the primitive facilities that have been offered to their menfolk for the past seventy years or more.

Critical interest in present-day soccer is of a high order. Match reports are allotted a great deal of space even in the weightier national newspapers and there is endless debate on the relative value of various tactical systems. At club level there is an inevitable and rarely satisfied demand for managers who are brilliant tacticians as well as shrewd businessmen. The old-style manager, once a famous player but otherwise unqualified to grapple with the complex problems of his new occupation, is on his way out. Most modern club managers *are* ex-players but only the cleverest, the most tactical-minded and the most businesslike continue to hold their jobs.

I suppose that as a race the British have a name for being born amateurs at sport. Foreign cartoonists are still likely to depict our cricketers as lean-faced aristocrats wearing Harlequin caps and white silk scarves to the wicket for a hearty knock; our footballers as baggy-shorted Corinthians out for an afternoon's spree in the mud; our lawn tennis players as earnest, tubby young girls fairly strong in the arm but lacking all subtlety; and our runners as university types who pull off one or two surprising wins in international competition and then fade out, to spend the rest of their lives as whiskey drinking stockbrokers.

In isolated cases, and at some time or another, this may have been true; but none of these caricatures bears any resemblance to the serious, hard-training young men and women who represent us in top-level sport today. Again, it is the sportsmen and sportswomen themselves who set the pace: no one forces them to compete, and to do all the training that is so necessary for participation in first-class sport.

Our national coaches, and the many coaches who give their services voluntarily to every sport, help to keep this new enthusiasm alive and to guide it into productive channels. It was not so long ago that coaching was frowned upon in most of our sports. Either you were a 'natural' sportsman and were paid some attention – or you were merely average and had to make your own way. Nowadays physical education as a profession is highly regarded and any boy or girl who shows the slightest promise at school is sure to have the benefit of expert tuition. Moreover, when he or she leaves school or university there is ample opportunity for further and more specialised training and coaching through courses arranged by local authorities, the governing body of a sport, the Central Council for Physical Recreation, or any other organisation dedicated to bringing on the young athlete. National recreation centres – the C.C.P.R administer five of them – are designed for the express purpose of providing serious training in a wide range of physical activities by expert coaches and instructors.

The facilities in a centre like Crystal Palace, designed and built by the G.L.C. (then the L.C.C.) and administered by the C.C.P.R., are as good as can be found anywhere in Europe; and the young people benefit immeasurably from being able to take residential courses, with the atmosphere of their sport around them day after day. The development of beginners in every sport is just as closely studied, but I am stressing what is being done at N.R.C.s for top-level sportsmen and sports-women because so often it is said that they are completely neglected.

To some, the word 'professional' has ugly connotations. But I believe it is a compliment for one's work to be said to have the 'professional touch'. And anyone who goes far along the road of serious competition in any sport *must* bear the impress of a professional – that is to say, dedicated – attitude to training and practice and accomplished performance. Whether com-pletely amateur sports like Rugby Union or hockey should admit professionalism in the sense of their best players being allowed to benefit financially from the sport is quite another matter and need not occupy us here. But it is worth reflecting that the decision to regard all cricketers as 'players' and to pay them or not to pay them, according to the wishes of the indivi-dual himself, does not seem to have brought any unpleasant elements into cricket.

It is this acceptance on the part of a sportsman that he must learn from qualified coaches how to improve his performance by means of proper training methods, a fairly rigid keep-fit schedule and constant practice, that is the bedrock of organised sport. The England team might never have won the World Cup in 1966 but for their manager and pilot, Sir Alf Ramsey, whom they so admired and respected.

Footballers are high-spirited young men, and when they are brought together as a group for pre-match training (the England squad stayed at Lilleshall Hall National Recreation Centre for the week preceding the World Cup-ties) there may be the odd player whose idea of beating the strain and tension atten-dant upon the prospect of performing before the eyes of the world is to 'have a good time'. This may mean no more than an evening at the local pub or late-night card sessions; but because Sir Alf has always believed in the importance of keeping one's mind on the task in hand, and so obviously would be upset by any such relaxation of athletic discipline, the England squad has never been troubled by outbreaks of this kind.

In consequence, when the players representing England go out on to the Wembley turf, or, come to that, on any foreign field, they are as fit and as highly tuned up as it is possible for footballers to be; and in July 1966 they proved themselves superior to the players of other nations not only in skill but also in stamina, fitness and the will to win. This was especially evident in the final when, after West Germany had scored an equalising goal in the last minute of injury time, they had to face another thirty minutes of play. Disappointed as they were to have given away a vital goal, they recovered magnificently and, playing as one man, eventually defeated the highly trained Germans who, themselves, played some unforgettable football.

So far as the actual government of a sport is concerned, how could we have borne the M.C.C. administration of cricket for so long if we were in revolt against authority? Who has ever heard of a major sport being administered by a private club! Yet it was only in 1967, and at the behest of the Minister for Sport, that an authoritative body was formed, called the M.C.C. Council, which will be empowered to deal with the Government on matters relating to the financing and development of the game. If I may labour the point, it is only in the late 1960s, the age of revolt, that a hitherto voluntary body has been given its statutory trimmings.

Naturally, team sports illustrate the acceptance or non-acceptance of authority and leadership much better than games where the individual is out on his own. In cricket, perhaps more than in any other team sport, the captain's control of his men in the field – or lack of it – determines whether or not the team will put up a good performance. It is for this very reason that the Test match selectors have to give so much thought to the appointment of an England captain; and if England loses a series, especially to Australia, it is the selectors' choice, as much as the captain's own playing performance, which the sporting press criticises, often rather savagely.

Have we any evidence that the cricketers of today make their captain's job harder because of any resentment of his position? Rarely has an England touring team pulled together so consistently and with such spirit as our team of 1965–6 under the captaincy of M. J. K. Smith. Yet the critics had given England very little chance against Australia in that particular series.

Some of the credit for their courage, determination and un-usually good form must surely go to the captain; and it follows, of course, that his leadership must have been accepted without question.

In the English summer that followed, England did badly against West Indies and, for the final Test at the Oval, Brian Close, Yorkshire captain and all-rounder, was plucked from the wings of international cricket, where he probably thought he would be staying for the rest of his playing career, to instil a fresh fighting spirit into the team. He took firm control of the game, inspired his men by taking vital catches at suicidal short-leg, and helped England to register their only victory in the series.

Possibly the secret of getting the best out of a team in any game is for the captain to be able to command respect, and for his skill, experience and tactical knowledge to be fully recog-nised. In cricket the captain is usually an older man, an expert in one of the specialist fielding positions, the captain of his county, and more useful as a batsman or bowler. In the past – and this points one of the main differences between pre-war and post-war sport – he was also an amateur. Until Len Hutton's appointment it had been considered unthinkable that England should be led by a professional. Those were the days of 'gentlemen' and 'players', the days when at Lord's the amateurs took the field through one gate, the professionals through another.

It could be said, therefore, that at that time authority was vested in a man's birth and upbringing. But it would be a dis-tortion of the truth to say that England captains were selected on these endowments alone. Their cricket had to match that of the professionals they were leading, and often they were among the best cricketers in the side; one thinks of P. B. H. May and F. R. Brown, D. R. Jardine and A. P. F. Chapman and J. W. H. T. Douglas. And even if we do believe that it must be better for sport for distinctions of class and education to give way to judgment based purely on experience and skill, we can still acknowledge the great performances of the past.

Sport, as we know it, owes a great deal to the men who loved it so much that they planted and nourished it wherever they went. That soccer is now played in every corner of the world is due largely to British colonists (a despised word in these days!) and to the soldiers and, latterly, airmen who, wherever they were stationed, marked out their pitches – on sand or gravel or baked mud if there were no grass – changed into some kind of football kit and made the people of other races wonder at their skill and enthusiasm in manœuvring a leather ball between two rough goalposts.

I have said before but would like to say again, and finally, that if respect for authority seems as strong and as willing as ever on the part of sportsmen and sportswomen, despite fiercer and more professional competition, despite a much tighter administration of games in all civilised countries and the acceptance of proper coaching in every form of sport becoming more widespread, it must be because participation in organised sport means that one voluntarily accepts a code of conduct and a set of laws or rules. This very acceptance is a source of pleasure and satisfaction to the sportsman, and the more anarchic the state of the world may be, the more firmly does he adhere to his own order.

Self-respect, not necessarily respect for authority as such, is the sportsman's answer to intolerance, dissension, drug-taking and licentiousness.

John Scupham

Formerly Controller of
Educational Broadcasting, B.B.C.
Author, *Broadcasting and the Community*
(Watts New Thinkers Library, 1967)

Power may rest on naked force. Authority claims as of right to determine men's actions or guide their thoughts. Since its forms are manifold, acceptance of its claims may mean willing submission to a man with a mission or to a legitimate government; to a new or a traditional moral imperative. New social departures, bringing new claims into being, come in time to be accepted as established and anonymous parts of the structure of society. They nevertheless have their origin in the vision of individual men and women.

Bertrand de Jouvenel has lucidly traced the process by which the personal authority of the creative pioneer comes to be transferred to the institution which he creates. The prestige of the founder confers prestige on his successors; loyalty to him becomes loyalty to the continuing institution and the idea it enshrines. Nowhere is the process better shown than in the history of the mass media.

Last year a vast audience was watching on television the man who set broadcasting on a secure basis as a power to be reckoned with; neither as a subservient instrument of government, nor as a mere branch of show business, but as part of the permanent and essential machinery of civilisation, with its own proper degree of autonomy. Few of those millions can have failed to discern in him an original force. Many of them, especially among the younger generation, felt it as a remote and alien kind of force, profoundly out of harmony with an age that is sceptical of the authoritative and quick to react against any hint of the authori-

202

tarian. Very few of them seem to have remembered that the B.B.C. was shaped by a young man, operating with a trenchant efficiency to which his ultimate success bore triumphant witness in a world very different from the world of the 1960s.

Over the nature of that success there still hangs a fog of ignorance and misconceptions. The Reithian régime is identified with the ascendancy of 'the establishment'. The propagandist image of 'Auntie B.B.C.' which bears little enough relationship to the facts of the post-war period is projected back into the pre-war era. The liberties that broadcasting now enjoys are hailed as the marks of deliverance from the timid and restrictive managements of the past.

The truth is otherwise. Reith in his prime was the very type of the creative innovator; a man possessed by an idea, and driving his followers hard, but himself hardest, to overcome the opposition of vested interests and the sheer inertia of society at large. Alone among his British contemporaries he saw the full possibilities of the broadcasting medium and saw that they needed freedom for their development. Mr. Kenneth Adam has corrected the record in one important respect. In answer to an allegation that the B.B.C. in its earlier days was terrified of infringing the rights of newspapers he has insisted that 'of all the battles Reith, as Director-General, fought for the recognition of broadcasting none was so prolonged, so consistent, so bitterly contested or so important as that for the free right to present news on the air at times and in a manner which suited the B.B.C. and not the newspaper proprietors', and has told how Reith, 'with the persistence of which only he, even against some of the toughest negotiators in the country, was capable', finally secured that right.

In every branch of broadcasting the story is the same.

Ignoring the blinkered and complacent indifference of the Board of Education, Reith started a service for schools: wearing down at last the opposition of the Foreign Office he was allowed to start an overseas service. Throughout the first formative years from 1922 to 1926 it was the Post Office that turned down his persistent requests for permission to widen the area of debate and bring the great political issues of the day to the microphone. It was Reith who staged a debate on Communism with a Communist participant in 1923; Reith who walked a razor's edge during the General Strike, when one section of the Cabinet wished to take over the B.B.C., and who managed to maintain a reasonably objective service of news although he could not obtain permission, as he wished, to broadcast the Labour point of view. It was Lord Riddell, representing the press, who argued in 1925 to the Crawford Committee, set up to consider the future of broadcasting, that there were many subjects inherently unsuitable for treatment at the microphone since they would be 'highly objectionable to a large section of the community', and instanced birth control. It was Reith who pencilled in the margin of the memorandum the simple words, 'Give both sides'.

The leader of a task force manned by volunteers must set before them clear and compelling objectives. For Reith the end in view was never in doubt. It was the establishment of broadcasting as a means of public service. The volunteers, as Eric Maschwitz remembers them, were at first 'a bevy of ex-soldiers, ex-actors and adventurers which a Carton de Wiart, a C. B. Cochran, even a Dartmoor Prison Governor might have found some difficulty in controlling'. On the ablest of them and on their successors Reith imposed the authority of an idea. One of them, Rex Lambert, a radical and an individualist who never felt easy under Reith's personal dominance and who rocked the Corporation by a defiant assertion of the rights of the individual, nevertheless wrote of these early years that, 'You felt it a privilege to be in at the birth of such a mighty experiment – an experiment not only in the use of a new invention, broadcasting, but in its use for communal ends rather than for private profit.' There was, he felt, 'no limit to the devotion of the employees of the B.B.C. many of whom gave their whole time and thought, at leisure as well as in the office, to the future of the service'.

Intellectual certainty, passionate conviction and an inflexible will are not always easy to live with. They are often and intimately allied with the autocratic temper of a Reith or a C. P. Scott. They nevertheless have a cutting edge that is denied to the more urbane social virtues. Those who possess them are armed with that natural authority which is the necessary condition of every new enterprise that calls for collective action.

A merely personal authority can offer no guaranteed future to a seminal idea. Reith was never prepared to leave the future of public service broadcasting to the accidents of management. His self-imposed task was completed only when he had inspired and watched over that transition from a private company to a public corporation and that conversion of personal authority into duly constituted authority which have given this country its most powerful means of mass communication.

In theory there is a clear distinction between broadcasting and all the other mass media. Since wave-lengths are in short supply the State must licence and regulate their use, whereas anybody may start a newspaper. In practice newspaper finances have reached a point at which Lord Thomson doubts whether all of our present national dailies can survive. We blindly choose to believe that more and more of the great organs of opinion can safely be brought under the sway of one great newspaper empire provided only that the present emperor is indifferent to the great public issues of the day and cares for nothing but money. In these new circumstances of sharply restricted access to the great public it is all the more vital that the B.B.C. should have been established as 'a trustee for the national interest' and should have taken the form of a public corporation – the first great national undertaking of the kind.

It was so designed that it should neither be free to exercise the harlot's privilege of power without responsibility nor be rigidly bound to the chariot wheels of the State. The United States predictably exerts the necessary minimum of public control. The logic of a competitive commercial system ensures that the American public shall be regaled from many sources with mud-wrestling one year, vampires another and vacuous soap-opera all the time. The Russian government possesses and uses in broadcasting the most potent instrument of propaganda. Britain, thanks to Reith, has placed public service broadcasting in the hands of an authority which derives from and is accountable to the sovereign power but is not simply that of the government of the day. Commercial broadcasting is, in the last resort, controlled by another public authority.

The free society is a plural society, rich in enterprises and associations possessing an authority which is not that of the monolithic State. None of them are more vital to the continuance of a democracy than those that have the power to mould men's minds. The freedom of the press and the qualified freedom of the broadcasting organisations are the only guarantee that men and women will be made aware of the full range of social, political and moral choices that lies open to them. What then should be the role of authority in the sphere of opinion, whether it is the *de facto* authority of the great newspapers or the *de jure* authority of the B.B.C. and the I.T.A.? A newspaper may elect to support one political party or one way of thinking: there are other newspapers to correct the balance and the State has conferred on none of them any special status. The situation of broadcasting is very different. The 1964 Television Act empowers the Independent Television Authority to control the national networking arrangements of the programme companies and enjoins it 'to secure a wide showing for programmes of merit'. The B.B.C. has been allotted two of the only four television channels which are likely to be available for many years, and a monopoly of radio. Between them the television programmes broadcast under the aegis of the I.T.A. and B.B.C. reach some 35 million people every day and occupy on an average more than two hours of the time of each of them. The B.B.C. and the I.T.A. share exclusive rights in a medium with a coverage greater that that of all newspapers combined but calling, like any newspaper, for the constant exercise of editorial judgment.

The power-structure through which that judgment is exercised is threefold. At the summit of the hierarchy there stand the reserve powers of Parliament which retains, as it must, the ultimate right to sanction, to prohibit and to guide and which can always vary through new legislation the terms on which it delegates its authority. When commercial television in Britain was sliding down towards the abyss of the sensational, the trivial and the narrowly monotonous in which American television lies, the government of the day thought fit to strengthen the hand of the I.T.A. and give it powers that the ethos and habit of a free-enterprise economy have always denied to its American counterpart, the Federal Communications Commission.

Next come the two public bodies with the large delegated powers conferred on them respectively by the B.B.C. Charter and the 1964 Television Act. On them rests full responsibility for the programme output, in sum and in detail. Lord Normanbrook, the last Chairman of the B.B.C. Board of Governors, was at pains to make it clear that this was no cipher responsibility, that the Board was 'the final source of decision, not only on general policy, but on specific issues which are of sufficient importance to call for decisions at the highest level within the Corporation', and that it was 'responsible for maintaining the moral and social values which should characterise good public service broadcasting'. It was, he explained, his own personal decision not to renew an invitation to Mr. Ian Smith, as Prime Minister of Rhodesia, to appear in the programme, 'Twenty-Four Hours'. The Independent Television Authority is required to ensure that the programmes broadcast under its aegis 'maintain a high general standard in all respects, and in particular in respect of their content and quality and a proper balance and wide range in their subject matter'. The memory is still fresh of the vigorous action which Lord Hill, the last Chairman of the I.T.A., took to carry out his brief and of the consternation to which it gave rise among those whose broadcasting franchises were withdrawn, curtailed or modified.

The powers of the I.T.A. and B.B.C. (bearing in mind that the Board of Governors are, legally, the British Broadcasting Corporation) must, in practice, be judicial powers. They are arbiters rather than originators. From the formal point of view the Director-General of the B.B.C. is its chief executive officer. In fact he is and must be the principal legatee of Reith's function as creative pioneer and the initiator, subject to the decisions of the Board, of new policies. Some time ago a television critic wrote of the vogue for satire, 'We can, however, be reasonably certain of one thing. The programmes were neither inspired nor encouraged from above.' Sir Hugh Greene was moved to write in reply that 'if ever in the history of broadcasting there was a programme which was both inspired and encouraged from above it was "That Was the Week That Was" '.

In the world of journalism there need be only one level of command. Lord Thomson would have us believe that within his empire the judgment of each individual editor is supreme, provided only that the paper pays. There may by two levels under a crusading proprietor, a Northcliffe or a Beaverbrook, both of them personal in character. In broadcasting there are necessarily three levels if it is to serve a democracy: the State, the autonomous public body and the creative executive. At every one of those levels there is an inescapable need for firm and final decisions. The next available channel must be allotted to one or another of the interests competing for it; permission to go ahead with a controversial new departure must be given or withheld; direction – and sometimes impetus – must be given to the multifarious projects competing for limited air-time and limited broadcasting resources. Irrevocable choices must be made between them.

The conduct of the mass media calls constantly and inevitably for the exercise of authority to enforce acts of choice. Choices can be made only in the light of values. Neither broadcasting nor the press can mirror the contemporary world. A mirror shows all that confronts it in the proportions presented to it. Even if such an image could be offered it would be intolerably dull. Neither broadcasting nor the press can aim merely at satisfying public demand or 'giving the people what they want'. As with other consumer goods, the great and largely inarticulate audience responds to what is set before it. Any purely commercial enterprise is engaged in creating a taste for those goods which it can most readily and profitably supply. The criteria of choice can be mercantile. The result, in broadcasting, can be only the maintenance of the maximum possible audience for the longest possible time through an appeal to the highest

common factors of taste and discrimination among an ill-edu-
cated general public – and it must always be remembered that
nearly three-quarters of the population left school before the
age of fifteen. In that process the present interests of minorities
and the future possibility of enriching life by an extension of
interests for the many are alike sacrificed.

A second range of criteria can be orientated not towards
profit but towards survival. The temptation of any large
organisation is to believe that its mere survival is an end in
itself. It is a temptation to which the B.B.C. was deliberately
exposed by the introduction of commercial television. Since
then, as Reith foresaw, the tyranny of statistics has steadily
extended its sway. Survival is an obvious prerequisite of service.
Public service broadcasting must command the respect and
allegiance in some sense of a majority of the nation. To identify
that means to an end with the maintenance throughout the
evening of a gross audience larger than that of the commercial
rival by competing with it on its own ground is to surrender
and not to gain authority. To court popularity for the wares of
a second channel by advertising them as wholly undemanding,
the customary offerings of show business, is either a false claim
or an abdication. So long as the audience research figures
continue to proliferate in a grotesque profusion of competitive
detail and to be taken as a guide to policy, the B.B.C. will find
itself more and more involved in the rationalisations which
represent the establishment of a 'pop' music channel as a blow
for cultural democracy and the cult of violence as a courageous
reflection of our troubled era.

Beneath the surface, however, the older tradition obstinately
survives: the tradition which insists that broadcasting, to use
the words of the Pilkington Report, 'is and will be a main factor
in influencing the values and moral standards of our society',
and that the authority of a broadcasting organisation in the
outside world must derive neither from figures nor from popular
clamour but from its own sense of standards. Indeed, if it were
not so, and if the B.B.C. set its course wholly by the standards
of the market place it would be impossible to justify its continuance with special privileges side by side with commercial
broadcasting.

o

Public service broadcasting is the exercise of a delegated authority to serve the common good; but who shall decide in what the common good consists? The great newspaper editor can set himself limited goals and pursue them with the passion of a partisan. Broadcasting, with its charge from the State to inform, to educate and to entertain, touches life at many more points yet is debarred from espousing any cause that divides men on political lines or lies outside the broad area of consensus. It must try to discern in our divided and changing society the long-established and the emergent needs that it can best satisfy. Its scope is too great, its responsibility too various for any approach that carries with it overtones of the autocratic, the dictatorial or the egotistical. Within the organisation itself and towards the community it serves the conduct of broadcasting must offer the very type of a democratic use of authority.

If a broadcasting organisation is to be aware of present needs and possible future interests in all the fields that it embraces; if it is to realise the full potentialities of the media that it commands as channels for the creative arts; if, above all, it is to maintain 'a constant and sensitive relationship with the moral condition of society', as the Pilkington Report said it should, that can be only through the whole host of men and women whom it employs as well as through its governing body. There is no way of dictating to the public what its interests should be, or of commanding creative ideas to emerge, or good programmes to be written. Each producer, with his personal contacts, his individual sensibility, his special knowledge and his own powers of judgment must be allowed his own sphere of authority and must contribute to the building up of the general framework within which his authority is exercised. Each head of department must carry his full share of delegated responsibility for the sorting out of ideas, projects and proposals. He can do so effectively and with understanding only if he thinks of his work as a continuing dialogue with his staff issuing in provisional conclusions on which he must act but which must in turn be so presented to his own superiors that they contribute to a larger pattern of decision making. At every level decisions must be made – and made by individuals. At every level they build up into a body of case-law and of implicit or explicit principle, an expression of purpose and of values which offers clearer guidance than any hortatory statement could. At the highest level within the organisation the tacit or the expressed approval of the Board of Governors – or the Authority – endorses them as acts of policy.

At this level policy has, of course, contributory sources that are wholly independent of the process of communication upwards within the broadcasting organisation itself. The perennial temptation of the organisation is to think that process all-important, to overvalue its own professionalism and to close the ranks against criticism from outside. The duty of the governing body is to ensure that its members bring to bear on their task their personal experience in the worlds of thought, of politics and affairs, the views of general and special advisory bodies and the preponderant weight of responsible opinion in the community. Mrs. Mary Whitehouse and her National Viewers and Listeners' Association would like to see them supported here, as they are in many other countries, by a council representing the views of consumers. It is certain that broadcasting can achieve the purposes of a democracy only in so far as that democracy exerts steady and active pressures upon it. The churches, the trade unions, the teachers' associations, the professional bodies and the universities should all be deeply concerned with broadcasting as a mode of public communications that profoundly affects them and their interests and that ought to be sensitive to their needs, views and wishes.

It may still be doubted whether any new body could efficiently carry out any supervisory or watchdog function for which there is not already an adequate provision provided only that it is vigorously used. No organisation or combination of organisations can speak comprehensively for the common listener and the common viewer. No committee representing sectional interests could usefully sit round a table weighing one of them against another or arrive at a balanced overall view of the enormous and multifarious programme output. Only a reasonably small group of people meeting often enough to arrive at a common mind and armed with all the powers necessary for ultimate control could ever be in a position to lay down a general policy based on a realistic assessment of the possibilities and therefore capable of offering firm guidance to the executive. The responsibility for bringing the purposes of broadcasting into full harmony with those of the community that it exists to serve must rest squarely with the statutory governing body. On what considerations, then, can it rest its claims to authority?

It must once more be emphasised that the position of broadcasting is different from that of the press. The authority to which both of them aspire is an admitted right to sway men's minds. For both of them that right must rest on a patent and disinterested concern for the common good, pursued with the intellectual integrity which C. P. Scott once described in a passage whose final sentence has become a *locus classicus*: 'The newspaper is of necessity something of a monopoly. Its primary office is the gathering of news. At the peril of its soul it must see that the supply is not tainted. Neither in what it gives, nor in what it does not give, nor in the mode of presentation, must the unclouded face of truth suffer wrong. Comment is free, but facts are sacred.'

A newspaper can nevertheless adopt a cause. A broadcasting organisation, with its quasi-monopoly powers conferred on it by the State and with a scope that extends far beyond its news services, is under the restraint of impartiality. 'In general terms', as Sir William Haley put it, 'broadcasting has the responsibility to be impartial on all subjects on which there is not common consent.' But, as he went on to say: 'The crux of the matter is to decide what is common consent.' The problem becomes infinitely more difficult in an age of rapid change like ours when the area of consensus is constantly shifting.

From time to time there have been considered attempts to map that area in the most general terms as an area of moral consensus.

For Reith its limits were set by a firm Christian commitment. 'Christianity happens to be the stated and official religion of the country', he wrote. For Sir William Haley there were distinctions to be drawn between the Christian values and the Christian faith and, while there was a proper place within broadcasting for Christian evangelism, it was no part of the general duty of the B.B.C. to make converts. Broadcasting, however, was not neutral where Christian values were concerned. 'There are many demands of impartiality laid upon the Corporation,' he told the British Council of Churches in 1948, 'but this is not one of them. We are citizens of a Christian country and the B.B.C. – an institution set up by the State – bases its policy upon a positive attitude towards the Christian values. It seeks to safeguard those values and to foster acceptance of them. The whole preponderant weight of its programmes is directed to this end.'

Two years later the Corporation, in its submissions to the Beveridge Broadcasting Committee, re-affirmed its allegiance, not explicitly to Christian values nor indeed to any specific values, but to the concept of a hierarchy of values and the need for continuities as well as for change: 'We live in one of the great transitional periods of history. The part that broadcasting can play in determining the shape of things to come must not be overestimated. But wisely constituted, responsibly conducted, guided and inspired both internally and externally by a sense of its responsibilities, there are some services it should be able to render. Not the least of them is to be a bastion against the tide seeking to submerge values in a disintegrating world.'

For Sir Hugh Greene in 1965 the older certainties were already a thing of the past. Broadcasting must beware of attaching 'a ubiquitous, unanswered question mark to everything – in religion, culture, politics or education'; it should not be neutral 'in clear issues of right and wrong'; nevertheless, 'the main purpose of broadcasting is to make the microphone and the television screen available to the widest possible range of subjects and to the best exponents available of the differing views on any given subject; to let the debate decide, or not decide, as the case may be'. The B.B.C. and other broadcasters should 'encourage the examination of views and attitudes in an atmosphere of healthy scepticism', and recognise 'an obligation towards tolerance and the maximum liberty of expression'.

Confronted with views so divergent, and even more with their fruits in programme output, the public can reasonably ask whether the whole basis of our culture has been radically transformed within a period of twenty years; to what extent the accident of changes in the managerial control of broadcasting has modified its role in society; and where the broadest area of consensus as a basis for policy now lies.

It is clear that a straightforward appeal to the Christian faith and Christian values is no longer valid for an increasing number of the men and women on whose support broadcasting must rely as members of staff, as contributors and as informed and active representatives of public opinion. Lord Hill has recently affirmed as an act of B.B.C. policy that Christianity, as one of the formative forces in our civilisation, should continue to hold a privileged position in broadcasting which cannot be claimed by any single Humanist doctrine. But within the context of general programmes every kind of belief or lack of belief finds a place.

Tradition no longer claims a wide acceptance as tradition, but only in so far as particular traditions are individually acquitted at the bar of reason or seen in their sum total to make their contribution to the coherence and well-being of society. How, then, does the doctrine of challenge to tradition stand up to the same rational scrutiny?

In so far as it recognises the present pace of social change, the gulfs that change opens up between one generation and another, the diversity of views in our society, the constant need for a revision of codes and a reconsideration of their foundations, and the paramount importance of free speech and wide-ranging debate in the preservation of an open society, it is inexpugnable. In so far as it understates the element of judgment involved in the choice of programmes for broadcasting it begs too many questions. To admit 'the widest possible range of subjects' is still to exercise a rigorous process of selection and exclusion. To choose a Reith lecturer – and in my own time few decisions were taken with more deliberate care – is to endorse one point of view rather than another as having a special urgency and significance.

Last year's series might indeed have been chosen to illustrate by caricature the implications of any social doctrine that exalts the quest but doubts the goal. From facts familiar enough to Montaigne but freshly endorsed with the imprimatur of the structural anthropologist, Dr. Leach hustled us with something less than Montaigne's care for logic towards the assertion that no agreed moral consensus is possible in our changing society yet somehow smuggled 'biases in favour of humanitarian values' – unspecified but regarded as self-evident – into his argument as having a quasi-moral claim on everyone. In their name he called upon an unspecified 'us' who appeared sometimes to be the scientists among us and sometimes, *per impossibile*, the general public to whom he was talking, to take control of 'our' destinies by unspecified actions for unspecified purposes, except that we should strive towards a state of 'permanent revolution' and universal tolerance.

No doubt, Dr. Leach's is a voice that should be heard, if only because it finds a ready echo among the urban intelligentsia. Whether it commands any wider assent as the basis of a philosophy of society and of broadcasting is more doubtful. If men's moral beliefs are, as Dr. Leach holds, determined wholly by their circumstances; if they are no more than an expression of group interests, there is no reason why I should extend to them when they conflict with my own interests and beliefs that toleration they can claim if we are all engaged on a quest by different routes for attainable common beliefs and convictions.

> *'Things fall apart; the centre cannot hold;*
> *Mere anarchy is loosed upon the world.'*

To accept the maximum freedom of expression as leading inevitably to the maximum diversity of opinion is to acquiesce in the consummation that Yeats foresaw. The alternative is to look for purposes that are capable of uniting Christians and humanists together with all those who, on simple pragmatic grounds, believe that no community is likely to survive and prosper without any principle of cohesion and to use broadcasting as one of their most powerful instruments. Perhaps, after all, they can still be found in the central traditions of public service broadcasting itself. The best sanction for the authority of the mass media may have been formulated by the greatest of their pioneers.

First, there is C. P. Scott's sacredness of facts; still sacred both inside and outside the great broadcasting organisations, though threatened at times by the encroachments of documentaries moving in a twilight zone between fact and opinion.

There is, as always, the intellectual integrity which ensures that the slanted argument is countered, that the scientifically disreputable reaches the microphone and the television screen neither in programmes nor advertisements; that the great public is neither denied the unorthodox nor hoodwinked by charlatans. There is the sense of balance – Reith's 'give both sides' – which recognises that in the dialectic of social change the voice of tradition and the voice of innovation have equal rights to be heard, however unfashionable or however disturbing the one or the other may be.

Beyond all these, beyond the regard for such truths as men know they can attain, there is the passion that truth shall prevail by being brought home to every man and woman in terms that they can understand. In so far as the mass media are sources of private profit their working assumptions may be those of Mr. Cecil Harmsworth King: 'It is only the people who conduct newspapers and similar organisations who have any idea quite how indifferent, quite how stupid, quite how uninterested in education of any kind the great bulk of the British public are.' In so far as they are trustees for the public interest it is not simply a prudential concern for the future of democracy but a moral concern for human worth that must range them on the side of Reith's 'It is better to over-estimate the mentality of the public than to underestimate it.' Everything we now know about the distribution of human ability bids the mass media to range on the side of the educational revolution of our times not simply a specialised educational sector of the output but, as Reith believed, the full weight of the general programmes.

Tastes differ. That simple fact has not yet convinced most of those who care for the arts that there is no scale of values within them. There is patently a community of tastes and of interests among those who have been lucky in their education which those who have not been so lucky cannot share. Northcliffe's 'Never put on the plate of Demos what you would not put on your own' is perhaps a counsel of perfection for the masters of the mass media: but it is only in counsels of perfection that

that authority finally and unimpeachably resides. If the mass media can hold a truly open forum for the great debate of our time and if they can contribute to the forging of a common culture as a basis for common values, their service to society may give them an authority which will be denied to them so long as their cultured right hand knows but does not care what their rating-conscious left hand does.

P

Sir Colin Coote, D.S.O.

Formerly Editor of the *Daily Telegraph*

It is an ingrained belief among the British public and politicians that newspapers have a profound effect in moulding opinion. Some statesmen, like A. J. Balfour, have asserted that they never read newspapers, but many whom I have known 'feather' after mention and comment in the press like hounds after the scent of a fox. Oddly enough, this favourable view of the influence of the press is held even more strongly in countries where democracy does not exist or no longer exists. The very first idea of a dictator of any sort of colour, red or black, is to nobble the press.

I had a personal experience of this forty-five years ago when I arrived in Rome as a British correspondent only a few months after the arrival of Mussolini. Mussolini was a journalist himself and, technically speaking, a good one. Yet he set himself deliberately to destroy all vestiges of independence in the Italian press. Amendola, Editor of *Il Mondo*, was set upon in the street and beaten up so badly that he died later. The Albertini brothers were ousted from the Milan paper, the *Corriere della Sera*, which they had raised to a high pitch of excellence. Thus I learned early that talk of the 'liberty of the press' is no cliché and that without liberty of the press there can be no liberty of anyone or anything. The critical faculty withers away and the mind becomes encased in a strait-jacket of official slogans. As for the still existing Communist dictatorships, *Isvestia* and *Pravda* are nothing more than technically competent gramophones for the Soviet Government.

It is worth noting that another kind of dictator, Général de Gaulle, has varied the technique. He has not bothered very much about the press, though it is, on the whole, generally

The Press

hostile to him. Possibly he knows that many French papers under the Fourth Republic became mere 'Feuilles de Chou' – 'Cabbage Leaves' – and that the status of the French press as a whole, though it had some brilliant writers and reporters, had gravely declined since the days of Clémenceau and Zola. But he has acquired complete government control of radio and television which was only temporarily and partially shaken by the near-revolution of May 1968.

Faced with this consensus of opinion about the importance of the press I suppose that I ought to say, as Richard Tauber used to sing in another context, 'Who am I to interfere with this?' And, indeed, it is extremely healthy that this opinion should prevail. But I must point out that it is only under certain conditions.

Take first the case of *The Times*, on which I served for twenty years. It is, of course, perfectly true that during the whole of Geoffrey Dawson's second editorship, from 1922 when the paper ceased to be 'a threepenny edition of the *Daily Mail*'* until 1939 when its policy of appeasement collapsed, *The Times* reflected the intimately gathered views of ministers. But how much it reflected and how much it moulded those views is uncertain. It was undoubtedly a far more effective moulder of public opinion in the days when the virulence of its attacks on governments earned it the title of 'The Thunderer' than when it was thought to be the voice of the Foreign Office. Its authority was much greater when it opposed than when it condoned. For example, one leader, 'Corridors for Camels', searingly and

* The phrase is Lloyd George's. Lord Northcliffe, his bitter enemy and owner of the *Daily Mail*, had bought *The Times* and used it to attack the Coalition Government. Northcliffe died about the same time as the Coalition collapsed and Dawson, whom he had displaced from the editorship, was brought back.

searchingly exposing the Hoare-Laval agreement virtually to surrender Abyssinia to Mussolini, bust the agreement and the Foreign Secretary and nearly brought down Baldwin who had condoned it.

A weakness of *The Times* was that, though all its staff writers were anonymous, quite a lot of people knew who they were. All my friends in the House of Commons knew that I wrote most of the political leading articles and, if they were critical, as they quite often were, would say to each other: 'Oh, it's only Colin letting off steam.' And, since the circulation of *The Times* was relatively tiny, the people who read it at all were few – it was more quoted than read.

Very much later, when the paper got into difficulties, it tried to recover ground by advertising that 'Top People Read *The Times*'. The claim was ill-conceived. It is the British middle class which has been really formidable for at least two generations or even, I could argue, for the best part of two centuries and it is to them in format, in contents and in price that a paper must appeal if it wants to be read and followed.

The real strength of *The Times* was its correspondence columns. The indignant had recourse to 'writing to *The Times*' almost as a matter of course. When the restive wanted to put a case they did the same thing. These letters from the eminent certainly did help to mould opinion. *The Times* no longer possesses the monopoly of such things that it used to have; but letters both in its columns and in those of other papers still exert a great influence.

Let me now turn to the *Daily Telegraph* on which I served for twenty-two years. Its success is due precisely to what I have just written – an enormous increase in the middle class or, if you prefer it, people with incomes at the £1,500 a year level. The number has much more than doubled in the last eight years. Did it and does it mould opinion? Well, here are some relevant comments.

If the *Daily Telegraph* had been, or had been thought to be, the mouthpiece of the Conservative Central Office its influence would have been small. As long ago as the time of the great Napoleon, the French Government published a sheet called the *Moniteur*, not a word of which was believed – at least outside

France – simply because it was official.* Any influence the
Telegraph possesses is basically due to its consistent insistence
on its independence. It expresses a Conservative philosophy
but that is by no means always synonymous with Conservative
policy.

A corollary to the distrust by the public of official voices is
that, if a newspaper wants to exercise influence on opinion, it
must be fair. Every nuance of views must be allowed in the
letter columns. Writers of differing political shades must be
given space in special articles. If a mistake is made it must be
corrected without fuss. The news must not be slanted. Then
people far outside the party the paper supports will begin to
read it. I can give no guaranteed figure for today, but I should
be surprised if the readership of the *Daily Telegraph* comprises
less than fifteen per cent of Socialists who take the paper to see
what reasonable opponents say. The figure given by the national
Opinion Poll in a survey published in December 1964 was
sixteen per cent, while seventeen per cent were non-Conser-
vative. There was a time that when a statement was challenged
the author could reply: 'It must be true, I saw it in the paper.'
Why should not that time return?

I have sometimes been asked why the late Lord Beaverbrook,
a first-class journalist, the autocrat of his technically excellent
publications and a fierce and fervent combatant for any cause
in which he believed, himself declared that he had never been
able to bring to success any political campaign. He was no
doubt thinking of the Empire Crusade and his futile vendetta
against Stanley Baldwin. A possible explanation was that his
moods were too vehement, his methods too violent. Pepper is
an excellent condiment but too much of it only makes you
sneeze. In any case, he was the principal actor in an affair
which showed how difficult it is to oust a politician, even though
strong support for the course favoured by the press spontaneously exists.

Beaverbrook had disliked Baldwin because the latter, though
he had been the chief architect of the demolition of Lloyd

* The extent to which Napoleon's pronouncements were deceptive is
illustrated in his letter to Marie Louise during the Russian campaign of
1812. They usually ended: 'My health is excellent. My affairs go very well.'

George, had caused Bonar Law some embarrassment – or so he thought. And Bonar Law had been Beaverbrook's idol. I was told at the time that Beaverbrook had been outraged by the way his beloved friend had been practically forced to accept the debt settlement which Baldwin had negotiated in the United States. Poor Bonar was moribund at the time and his struggle against cancer of the throat was drawing to a close; but genuine emotion knows no logic.

Anyhow, when Baldwin lost two out of three General Elections and would not swallow a revived version of Joe Chamberlain's 1904 campaign for an Empire Customs Union, Beaverbrook saw a chance to get rid of him. Defeat never does a leader's popularity any good. In addition, Baldwin was known to favour giving autonomy to India of a kind and at a pace which, in 1930, caused Churchill to resign from the Shadow Cabinet. Lord Rothermere, owner of the *Daily Mail*, the *Sunday Dispatch* and other papers, joined in the hunt. Baldwin seemed to be rocking in the saddle.

At that moment the sitting M.P. for St. George's, Westminster, died. He was Sir Laming Worthington-Evans, who had held high office in the Lloyd George Coalition, and the seat was a Conservative stronghold. The malcontents rightly calculated that if an anti-Baldwin candidate could be found and could win the seat, Baldwin would have to resign the leadership. They found a pleasant, elderly person, Sir Ernest Petter; and the general view was that the press would waft him in.

But Alfred Duff Cooper (afterwards Lord Norwich), a pugnacious character, who had won the hand of the pre-war reigning beauty, Lady Diana Manners, by winning a D.S.O. in the field, had other ideas. He had lost his seat in 1929 and was nursing Winchester. But the pro-Baldwin faction prevailed on him to stand for St. George's and, after a fierce battle for a fortnight, he won hands down, thus saving Baldwin and making his own career. He won, though the *Daily Telegraph* was the only paper which backed him. The rest varied from bitter hostility to cagy neutrality.

Baldwin turned this defeat of the press lords into a rout at a great meeting in the Albert Hall. They had been foolish enough to put on paper the conditions upon which they would support

him, which really would have given them the authority con-
stitutionally reserved to, and formerly exercised by, the Crown.
Baldwin said they were seeking power without responsibility,
'the prerogative of the harlot throughout the ages'. The phrase
was suggested by Baldwin's cousin, Rudyard Kipling; and it
had enough truth in it to be a knock-out.

The limits of the political influence of the press are so
important that I should, perhaps, give some more rather
striking examples of them. On the morrow of the colossal
Liberal victory of 1906, a new Liberal newspaper called the
Tribune was started. It was a complete flop, though the Liberal
Party was on the crest of a tidal wave.

More recently there was the career of the *Daily Herald*, the
official organ of the Labour Party. With such a title and such a
crowd of potential fans (there are, after all, 850,000 subscribing
members of the Labour Party and eight million trade unionists)
one would have thought that it was certain of success. Indeed,
its staff were often excellent. But nothing could make it do
better than stagger along until the invalid was taken over and
relabelled by a concern of a more sensational kind. Of course
the difficulties of many papers have been and are being caused
by the impossibility of increasing advertisement revenue to
meet rising costs.* But sometimes it seems that people buy
papers for the moulding of views about everything except
politics. It may do a paper more good to have a successful racing
correspondent than a very Solomon of a political commentator.

It is also necessary to remember that in the British electoral
system a little influence may mean a lot. In about two-thirds of
the 630 constituencies nothing but a landslide will change the
result of an election. The narrow Labour victory in 1964 was
won by a change in only seventy seats. But supposing in the
country as a whole there is a swing of as little as three per cent
from one party to another, there may be a change in between
fifty and a hundred marginal seats. So a newspaper has only
to change or mould the opinions of a handful of voters in a
handful of seats to affect the result of a General Election.

One further modern development may help the political

---

* If a newspaper had no advertising its economic price would be about
1*s.* 9*d.*

influence of the press. It is generally agreed that the era of the public meeting is fading out. Elections are won not on platforms but on doorsteps and in armchairs. The obvious reason is the almost universal use of the sound broadcast and of television. Undoubtedly television, particularly, is a political instrument of colossal weight. A political leader with a good television presence scores heavily.

But sound broadcasting was never really a rival of the press, though some newspapers foolishly refused to print B.B.C. programmes when it started. Listeners went to the press to see whether they had heard rightly. The combination of voice and view is certainly more impressive and convincing; but both are ephemeral whereas 'the written word remains'. Many doubters still want to consult it. Dr. Richard Rose in his *Influencing Voters* gives the audited figures of the circulation of the national press alone at about forty million at the end of 1964. This does not include anything for the provincial press, whose readership is also very large. The British are, indeed, voracious newspaper addicts and I don't think even TV will break their addiction. Many of my friends have told me of their reaction to the Niagara of politics poured out on TV during the 1966 election. There comes a time when there comes spontaneously to their lips the injunction, 'Turn the damned thing off'.

I doubt whether anybody has estimated or can estimate the effect of the various media of expressing political opinion on an electorate of over thirty million people. The Reform Act of 1832 holds pride of place in British political history but it added only about 250,000 to the total electorate and the Act of 1867 added only about one million more. The total in 1911 was about eight and a half million. Again, has anybody tried to estimate the effect of various forms of propaganda on women, who had no vote before the First World War, and now constitute more than half the electorate? Will the spread of secondary education lead to more interested pondering over politics or to more boredom with them? Will the projected grant of the vote to adolescents of eighteen make political conduct more mature or more volatile? The percentage of the electorate which voted even at the election of 1966, which was exciting enough, was the lowest since 1945.

The one development which would be fatal to the democratic system would be the spread of political apathy, of the view that no party is better than another and that none can do anything really effective. I am quite certain that the combating of political indifference is one of the main duties of a newspaper. Compulsory voting, such as exists in Australia, is no substitute for informed voting and, though there is such a thing as reasoned abstention, the extent of abstention from ignorance or lack of interest can be terrifying. Abstention ultimately does to politics what absenteeism does to industry. It is greater in the United States than here and some of the best American commentators have attributed some of the less agreeable features in American politics to the large part played both by public apathy and by professional ballyhoo. Are the press here to blame for similar symptoms?

For there *are* similar symptoms. Estimates of the percentage of the electorate who are really interested in politics range between fifteen and twenty percent. The interest of the rest is sporadic at best and non-existent at worst. I am not asserting that these figures reflect some deterioration in electoral quality. Indeed, I think the press gives a wrong impression of British youth by publicising that section of it which specialises in extravagances of action or of appearance. Look at the unprecedented crowds of industrious undergraduates or the remarkable dedication of young athletes. These characters are to be set against the occasional drug-addict or degenerate who makes the headlines. And very recently so-called students in many countries have given the impression that their favourite study is the technique of rioting. But if the press really set itself to make man more of a political animal it would not lack impressionable material.

Some papers still give some reports of parliamentary debates; but a paragraph of highlights, if any; a half-column about some intrinsically trivial scene and a political note or two are usually as much as are given or deemed newsworthy. This is largely Parliament's own fault. There are fewer 'characters' on the political scene; proceedings are too crowded for oratory or sparkling argument. Though the *Daily Telegraph* in my day kept, and still keeps, a relatively large coverage of Parliament, reports were not untruncated; but I never had any any request that they should be fuller – unless you like to count rather hurt messages from M.P. friends that their speeches had been omitted.

The moulding of opinion is not confined to politics. There are other fields in which the press takes a hand in shaping views. The largest is known in Fleet Street as 'culture' – a horribly precious term but not inapt. It includes literature, music, the theatre, painting and sculpture, architecture and even fashion. Every department of culture has its pitfalls. Reviewers of books are sometimes too inclined to demonstrate their own cleverness and erudition; but the proper purpose of a review is to say whether and why a book is worth reading at all. Music critics are apt to lapse into a jargon intelligible enough to specialists but not to the general public. The dramatic critic nearly always has a rush job to do in order to catch the main edition and great experience is required to do it well.

All forms of art are matters of opinion and there is no doubt that the opinion of journalists counts. Go past any theatre and look at the display of press comments, if favourable or capable of favourable interpretation, plastered outside. This is not to say that the critics are never wrong and can make or break a play or a musician. I have heard that Bizet's *Carmen* was torn to pieces by the critics at its first performance – not to give other, modern instances. The art critic's difficulty is that judgment of painting is a specially personal matter. Van Gogh was unable to sell a single painting in his lifetime. Whatever the personal predilections of a critic, he or she must try to understand why some forms of art – for example pointillism or surrealism – genuinely appeal to some people. It is wrong to dismiss such things as tripe, though perfectly legitimate to explain why one may think they are.

Remember that if you want a regular and detailed guide in such a large field it will be necessary to take in one of the specialist publications. But the well-known correspondents of daily or Sunday newspapers have a great following and the Sunday press, which tends to become more like magazines than newspapers, can and does devote much space to 'culture', often usefully. It might be invidious to single out the living, but the names of A. B. Walkley of *The Times* and Richard Capell of the *Daily Telegraph* may reasonably be recalled.

As for fashion, the able architects of what are known as 'Women's Pages' perhaps report more than mould opinion; though within such categories even as the mini-skirt they may help to create a certain selectivity. If they don't, it is not for want of trying, for there can be few topics that absorb more and glossier newsprint than female attire.

It would be superfluous to dive into the more recondite corners of journalism. This outline has, I hope, shown the extent to which the press sets up to be an authority. There is, however, a subsidiary question: namely, does it deserve to be an authority at all?

Its standards, like those of the politicians themselves, have often been challenged. Since the Second World War there have been two profound and prolonged enquiries into the standards and standing of the press. The first was set up by the post-war Socialist Government which, perhaps naturally, felt rather sore that so many newspapers were hostile. The complaints were made more specific by allegations that the newspapers were controlled by proprietors in their private and personal interests; that news was slanted; and that the methods of gathering news were indefensible. This conception that the press was an instrument of terrific potency wielded by bullying, tasteless, selfish and often foolish tycoons did not stand up to examination. Who did the critics desire should run newspapers? The Government? Disastrous! A committee? Impossible! The course of a critic who disapproved of the attitude or ethics of a newspaper was plain. He should stop buying it.

The outcome was the setting up of a Press Council to which complaints against newspapers could be referred. Just recently this body has been greatly strengthened by the inclusion as chairman of a high judicial personage – Lord Devlin. A proportion of complaints are bound to be frivolous and I cannot recall any in my time which were epoch-making. Editors and proprietors do not really spend their time trying to get away with unethical behaviour. If they did the law of libel would stop them expensively as often as not. Nevertheless, since most of the sensational press is or has been represented on the Council, this body has certainly done no harm. Perhaps it has done some good. Newspapers cater far less for the public appetite for the pornographic than they did at one time. It is an excellent omen that readers should prefer information to titillation.

The second trial of the press was mainly concerned with a different aspect of the matter. The inability to increase revenue enough to meet vastly increased costs proved fatal to two Liberal papers – the *News Chronicle* and the *Star* – and was later responsible for the sale of *The Times* to Lord Thomson of Fleet. The precarious financial condition of these and other papers caused people to wonder whether newspaper finance was well conducted or wasteful, and whether we were not getting too near the collapse of competition in certain categories of news-papers both national and provincial. The enquiry under Lord Shawcross confirmed what every journalist knew: that there was large scale overstaffing. This was partly due to restrictive practices. The Newspaper Proprietors' Association has always to negotiate with the unions under the special handicap that labour troubles inflict losses on the industry which cannot be recouped. If a paper misses an edition the proceeds are lost for ever. If a factory is shut for a day, the loss of production can be made good later. In America such troubles and astronomical increases in costs have driven some newspapers out of existence.

Lord Shawcross also found that no real danger of a monopoly was round the corner; and this was still the view when later the Monopolies Commission had to pronounce on the inclusion of *The Times* in Lord Thomson's portfolio. Lord Thomson is a new kind of element in the press. He consistently declares that the only part of it which interests him is the balance sheets. With the proviso that he is also interested in the prestige of owner-ship, the truth of this assertion has never yet been damaged by any interference with his highly qualified administrative staff. Other proprietors take an active part in running their papers – some more and some less. But not one in my acquaintance does so as an amateur. They are competently trained technicians and know very well that truth has many facets, so that policy is a matter of discussion not of dictation. The picture which critics sometimes draw of them as tyrants, browbeating unhappy editors and issuing ukases based solely on concern for their own interests is a complete caricature.

On the whole, therefore, the press stands acquitted of the charge that it is unfitted to have any authority over opinion. The British are not docile. Their natural reaction to authority is hostility and they are sometimes more inclined to stress what is faulty in their institutions than to boast of what is not. In my experience they are specially critical of the three Ps – Parliament, the Police and the Press; and yet these are probably the hardest working institutions in the land. Moreover, when it comes to a crunch, the public would not willingly dispense with any of the three. As the old rhyme says, in time of danger, 'God and the soldier is the cry'; but when the danger is past and wrongs are righted, 'God is forgotten and the soldier slighted'.

We have no reason to slight our press. It is true that a newspaper has to report salacious cases, otherwise the perpetrators could not be made into a warning. But I often thought that the parents who used to write that they dared not leave the papers containing such reports lying about for their children to read might be too timorous. Most children are older than their parents think! And in fact, having worked as a journalist in three countries, not counting missions to several more, I assert that British papers are the fairest, most accurate and most comprehensive in the world.

This view is, I know, not shared by those who have a natural dislike for the press for not sharing their views. One in this category is Lord Wigg, who used to be a sort of Minister without Portfolio to the Prime Minister in Downing Street. Mr. Wigg, it must be stated in fairness, never skimps his own home-work and when he takes up a case or a cause sweeps nothing beneath any carpet. He says that the relations between the press and the Government should not be too friendly but have become too acidulated. But whose fault is that? It is difficult to be buddies with secretive bores; and if government spokesmen won't tell what is happening, the duty of the press is to find out. Lord Wigg also says that newspapers curry favour with advertisers. He is probably thinking of the United States. In this country what curries favour with advertisers is the circulation figures coupled with the character of the readership.

There was never any improper wooing of advertisers on the paper with which I was connected but there was always a watch for, and a refusal of, improper advertisements. Again, Lord Wigg asserts that the press runs after stunts or scoops, not after facts. Possibly he is confusing journalism with politics. Anyhow, he has had, I believe, some contacts with the press. How does he think a paper could be a *news*paper if it spent as long investigating a case as a Royal Commission? It is to be feared that he still suffers from some of the illusions which two Royal Commissions discarded, for another of his criticisms is that the control of newspapers is concentrated in too few hands. As I have already said, that was not the view either of the more recent Royal Commission or of the Monopolies Commission. In short, it would greatly enlarge Lord Wigg's knowledge of what he is talking about if he spent, say, a week at a sub-editor's desk in the *Daily Telegraph*. He obviously has not the slightest idea of the trouble and expense devoted to the publication of news stories. They are comparable, though they cannot last quite as long, as those devoted to the preparation of feature articles. There are many correctives to unethical journalism such as a newspaper's own standards, which are quite as honourable as those of any Honourable Member, and the law of libel, but Lord Wigg's comments are not among the number to which anybody examining the extent of the influence of the press need pay much attention.

I must insert an obsession of my own. Other languages have their points and journalists will not find it useless to read and speak them. But the English tongue is a mighty instrument, strong and musical, with many complexities of spelling but few of declension or conjugation. In language, as in currency, there is a Gresham's Law – the bad tends to drive out the good. Don't let Americanisms creep into English prose. Don't show off by dragging in phrases in classical or modern tongues when English will serve. Bar official circumlocutions – for example, 'of the order of', when a plain adverb such as 'about' or 'approximately' is available. Naturally, I hope that the press will mould many things, but I passionately desire that it should mould English, and it is indeed distressing to hear a debased and uncouth piece of writing referred to as 'journalese'. I trust the meticulous reader will not find too many passages in which I have failed to practise what I preach.

I close with a reminder of how the view of the press by people in public life has changed. I am indebted to my friend T. F. Lindsay, so long a parliamentary sketch writer, for reminding me of that. There still exists, unrepealed but long ignored, a resolution passed by the Commons in 1738, which shows the snarky view of pressmen in those days: 'that it is a high indignity to, and notorious breach of the privilege of this House, for any news writer . . . to presume, to insert in . . . letter or papers or to give therein any account of the debates or other proceedings of the House . . . as well during the recess, as the sitting of Parliament; and this House will proceed with the utmost severity against such offenders'.

That reflects not so much the rascality of the press as the sensitivity of Parliament. How different today, when every M.P. is quite delighted at any notice whatever in the press and when every politician knows that it is better to be damned than unrecognised! Such is the mutability of human opinion! When the press, it seems, was capable of moulding opinion, our legislators snubbed and ostracised it. Now that its power, if not vanished, has certainly diminished, they court and cherish it.